Love is No Guarantee

Essential Ingredients to Creating A Successful Relationship

PETER HECTOR

Crunchbird Publishing

 For more information: Crunchbird Publishing, 8 Eastern Parkway, Newark, NJ 07106,

Library of Congress Control Number: 2002096796

Find us on the World Wide Web at:
www.loveisnoguarantee.com

Cover design by Randy Schultz
DesignPro Graphics

Interior Design by Irene Archer

ISBN # 0-9726221-0-1

Manufactured in the United States of America.

Dedication

To my wife Diomira, whose love has taught me the meaning of peace and happiness. You have been the inspiration for this book.

&

In memory of my father
Richard A. Hector Sr. 1906 - 2001

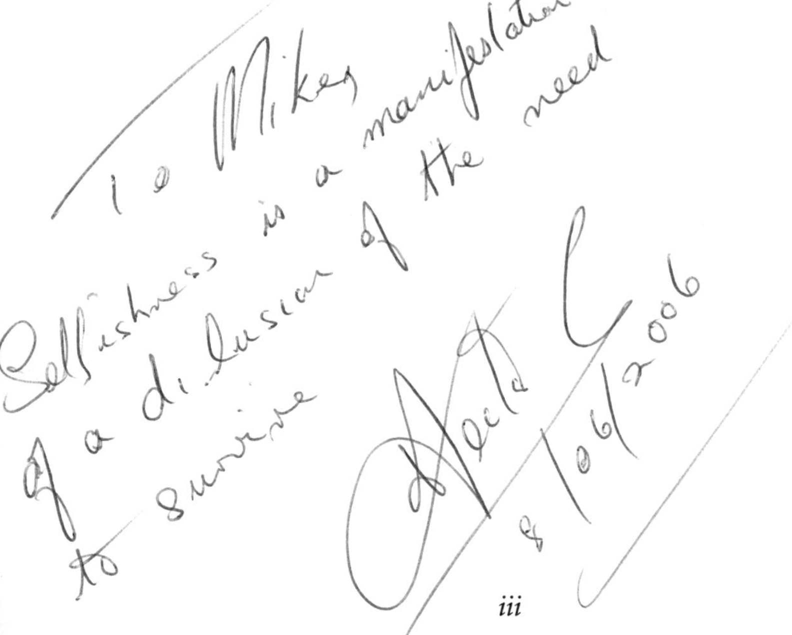

Acknowledgements

I wanted to create a book for people who want to find happiness and fulfillment in their love relationship. It had to be a book they would read and keep within close reach for easy reference. —Indeed, an enormous undertaking. However, the development and completion of this project would not have been possible without the people who gave their enthusiastic support.

A round of applauds for the people who agreed to be interviewed, and for those who willingly shared their most intimate experiences. Thumbs up for all the members of the research team, especially Anna Calogero —Your input has been extremely valuable.

For research support, special thanks to Elaine Small, Shelly Smith, Frank Cavicchia, Terrence Smith, the folks at the *Option Network* especially Deborah Di Marsico, Mandy Evans, and Jennifer Hautman, the folks at Shorewood, Pam, Judilee, Esther, Tony Orecchio, and Stanley Edwards.

I am deeply indebted to Erika Armstrong for her dedicated efforts in proofreading and critiquing draft manuscripts. Also to Khaya Ngcakani for her valuable input and feedback.

Special thanks to my brother Steve Hector, and my sisters Elaine and Jackie for your continued support.

My gratitude to the researchers and writers whose works support the information in this book. And finally, Cheers to my editor Barbara McNichol. Your proficient editing skills were surpassed only by your dedication to this project. Thanks Barbara, you are the greatest.

I am forever indebted to all of you.,

PH.

Table of Contents

Introduction

One in every three first marriages in the U.S will end within ten years, and one in five will end within five years, according to a November 2001 report issued by Centers for Disease control and Prevention. The report "First Marriage Dissolution, Divorce, and Remarriage: United States," also notes that 43% of first marriages will end within 15 years. [1]

Although recent statistics paint a bleak picture of the future of marriage, it seems that most people have not totally lost faith in the institution itself. Also, newer studies have revealed that the statistics on the success of remarriages are even less encouraging; remarried couples divorce at an even higher rate than first timers. Yet it is not uncommon to see many divorced people remarry for a second and even a third time.

It should be no wonder that, despite the statistics so many people are willing to risk the heartbreak, sorrow, and economic losses resulting from failed marriages. People need companionship, and marriage has been the accepted structure for men and women to live with each other for as long as we can remember.

However, over the past few decades, the staggering increase in the divorce rate in America has left young people in doubt about the idea of marriage itself. Many have opted for the less traditional arrangement, i.e., living together without the benefit of the marriage vows. One U.S. Census report "Marital Status and living Arrangements, 1996", showed an 85% increase in cohabitation within the last decade alone. But does this ensure compatibility in marriage? [2]

According to numerous studies, the rate of failure in common law relationships is 50% higher than that of traditional marriages. So the question is: What can couples do to reduce the rate of failure in their own relationship? Even more significant questions are: What are the reasons for these failures in so many relationships. Why do people who want to share their lives together find it so difficult to sustain long term relationships with each other? [i3]

The answer to these questions and more is the focus of this book. One of the principal causes of the high casualty rate in marital relationships lies in the sources of our life- long teaching and information about marriages. Most of us are familiar with the emotional side of romantic love. Less commonly known are the biological connections to these emotions. Anthropologist Helen Fisher [4] (more about this in Chapter 7) has documented evidence that links the biological and chemical processes of our bodies to love and attachment between males and females.

In her study, Fisher notes that our bodies produce chemical substances known to cause attachment in humans. She suggests that nature has provided a way to bring couples together and keep them sufficiently motivated until the creation of offspring is accomplished. Additional clinical experiments link reduced levels of these "love-enhancing compounds" in the human body with the decline of passionate love and attachment between couples. Fisher believes that the reduced levels of these chemicals may be directly responsible for separation and divorce in romantic relationships.

Most young people entering a relationship for the first time are not sure what is expected of them to be a good partner. The majority of the people we interviewed admitted they were not looking very far into the future when they got married. All they knew was that they were in love with someone who met their social and sexual requirements-at least the way they saw them at the time. For most of us, our parents have been our only source of first-hand information about marriage. But times have changed; what may have worked for our parents in their time may not work for us today. And with the high rate of failure reported in present-day marriages, it would seem unwise for us to use past-day examples of marriages as role models for our own relationships. We need to find better solutions.

Love is No Guarantee guides you through the process of finding love and keeping it alive in the face of today's challenges. It is not a book about psychology. I am not a psychologist and this is not an attempt to psychoanalyze why people behave the way they do; numerous well-qualified professionals have already done an excellent job in that area. This is a look at the practical, logical reasons for people's actions and the resulting consequences.

Part one covers all aspects of dating; guiding you to some of the places you can meet eligible people who share similar interests with you.

When you feel you are attracted to someone, *Love is No Guarantee* walks you through the steps you must take before you fall in love; yes, that's right, *before* you fall in love. Even when you believe you've found the right person, you will have to take steps to make certain "what you see is what you are getting."

For example, I've heard men complain they fell in love with women they met in a work environment. These men were attracted to and sought women who held interesting jobs and led socially stimulating lives. Imagine the surprise to those who married these women, only to discover that their wives want to give up their careers to become stay-at-home moms. Usually the relationship becomes strained because the men may feel they have been misled. Likewise, a man who is financially well off may marry a career woman but secretly plans to convince her to give up her career and become a housewife or a "trophy" wife.

When you do decide to choose someone you believe may be right for you, this guide suggests ways to confirm your initial feeling. You will be able to determine if, in fact, you can share a life together. These steps are relatively simple to follow, yet many people bypass them only to have regrets later. Remember, to enjoy a fulfilling relationship even with someone you love, you must share compatibility in the important areas of your life. You'll stand a better chance of understanding your partner if you both share similar values, personal habits, and opinions. You don't have to agree on everything; being in total agreement with your partner at all times can produce boredom in the relationship. In fact, even on some important matters, you can have different opinions. But at least you should see eye-to-eye in matters critical to your day-to-day existence.

For example, if you grew up in a wealthy family and have always appreciated, enjoyed, and looked forward to the finer conveniences of life, you may have difficulty living with a mate whose philosophy is to live on the bare necessities, especially if he or she believes accumulation of wealth is immoral. However, your relationship may still survive if you vote Republican and your partner is a staunch Democrat.

Love is No Guarantee explains what men and women want from each other in a relationship and how you can determine what your prospective partner expects from a relationship with you. Being aware of each other's expectations gives each person a clear picture about the other's willingness and ability to meet his or her needs.

When you are reasonably satisfied that the mate you chose is "the one" and you decide to formalize your relationship, Part

Two provides valuable tips to make your relationship a success. This may be even more important than it seems because the challenges we face on a day-to-day basis can cause us to neglect our relationships. And by the time we realize our mistake, it might be too late to repair any damage caused.

You will learn:

- What men really want
- What women really want
- How to tell if your partner truly loves you
- How to maintain love and intimacy while raising a family
- How to communicate your most intimate needs to your partner
- How to maintain a satisfying sexual relationship with the one you love
- How to deal with in-laws without loosing your hair
- The reasons why love dies

Love is No Guarantee teaches you to recognize signs that indicate potential trouble spots in your relationship before they get out of hand.

Each relationship has its own problems but many share similarities. It is my wish that you use the knowledge and experiences gained from others to seek solutions that can benefit you. It is my sincere hope that you can sit back, look at your own situation, and ask yourself whether your beliefs, expectations, and actions so far have worked for you. If so, congratulations! If not, you may want to adopt some of the practical applications outlined in this book to improve your own relationship.

This book is for people who want to find peace and happiness in their love relationship.

Prologue
The Future of Relationships

Is there any good reason to get married today? Can one be realistically expected to stay married to the same person for the rest of one's life? Whose idea was it to get married in the first place?

These questions might seem frivolous to some, but when we look at the increasing numbers of failures of marriages in our society today, it should come as no surprise that people everywhere are questioning the merits of the institution of marriage, an institution that has served as the foundation of our society for generations.

According to the Statistical Abstract of the United States, the overall numbers of marriages in the United States is increasing. Yet the divorce rate is steadily increasing (200 percent within the last 30 years). Today, it is estimated that over 50 percent of marriages end in divorce. [5] Every day people around us are in the process of splitting up. The situation gets worse if we consider the numerous cases in which relationships have technically ended, but the couples remain together because it's convenient to do so. These partners have long ago distanced themselves from each other, but social, economic, and other reasons keep them together.

Also, the findings of a recent Rutgers University study reveal an even bleaker picture for the institution of marriage. The report titled "State of Our Union" [6] indicated that (1) Over the past 40 years, many couples do not choose marriage as their first living-together experience and as a status of parenthood. (2) There has been a tremendous increase in the number of children born out of wedlock, which has increased the number of children who grow up in fragile families. (3) Even with the increased freedom to leave a marriage by divorce, high percentages of the remaining marriages are still unhappy.

In a confidential survey carried out in the United States and Canada, [7] people were asked to describe the state of their marriage or love relationships. Though not surprising the majority of answers received are unsettling to our society.

Rick, a department store security chief, said, "If I knew then what I know now, I would not have gotten married in the first place."

Andre 29, a clerical worker, said, "Women seem to be so nice when you first meet them. After you're married, it's as though they become someone else. It seems like they show all their good points until you give them that ring, then 'Wham,' you begin to see their real characters."

Sandra, a beautician at a downtown salon, said, "We get along OK but my husband is not as romantic as he used to be, and the closeness we had is no longer there. When Stan and I first got married, we were really in love. We were so excited about our plans for the future. Now, I like my husband, we get along just fine, but we have our separate lives. I don't feel in love; we seldom have sex. It has been like this for years. I guess that's how marriage is supposed to be."

Many people have come to the conclusion that marriage

will never deliver on the promise of joy and happiness they were conditioned to believe. They are convinced that really great marriages exist only in Hollywood movies. Therefore people should accept this reality and be happy with what they have, because if you live under the illusion that yours would be the exception, you are sure to be disappointed.

People tend to begin relationships with the best of intentions. These people are genuinely in love and are fascinated by their plans and great expectations for a bright future. But as time passes by, these same people get confused. They watch with great disappointment the deterioration and ultimate collapse of their relationships. They are unable to understand the reasons for these collapses, hence are powerless to do anything to salvage the situation. This disillusionment is devastating and make them wonder if any love relationship can be expected to survive.

Some people have made many attempts at finding lasting romantic love relationships. After several failed endeavors, they are convinced that, like other fantasies, romantic love relationships are unattainable. Some women are convinced that most of the good, eligible men are already taken. The rest, they say, are too old, too young, too insensitive, and, in many cases, too set in their ways.

Men, on the other hand, might believe the reason women are still available is because they are either unattractive, too materialistic, or simply carrying too much baggage. Yet people continue to fall in love, driven by a passion that refuses to be extinguished. It's as if their natural instincts say if they can somehow find true love, they can look forward to long-lasting happiness. So why does this happiness continue to elude people? What is this force so powerful that seems to prevent them from realizing their innermost desires?

Relationships succeed or fail for many reasons. However,

since each relationship is unique, there can be no hard-and-fast solutions to the multitude of problems experienced by couples. Over time, psychologists have learned a great deal about how people relate to each other. Thanks to the many years of in-depth research, clinical experiments, and human psychological analysis, enough information is now available to assist people who really want to find solutions to their marital problems.

Surveyed Couples

In the preparation of this book, I studied hundreds of cases relating to couples who are now married, or have been married or in a love relationship. With the help of two assistants, I interviewed 254 people in the United States and Canada. Many of our surveys were conducted in person, but we also got a flood of responses from people contacted on the Internet. Our findings, though not scientific, led us to these overwhelming conclusions: [8]

- Overall, most people feel their lives would be more fulfilled if they could share it with a love companion.
- Many people spend a great portion of their lives in the quest for love. In a great many cases, they enter marriage for the wrong reasons.
- One of the major causes of dissatisfaction in life and unhappiness in society today results from failed unions between men and women.
- Truly understanding the reasons why so many relationships fail, gives people the ammunition necessary (a) to improve their current relationship with others, and (b) avoid the mistakes that bring about this failure, even before starting a new relationship.

Most experts in the field of marriage and relationship counseling agree that rigid formulae cannot be applied in the behavioral sciences. This means that every case has to be treated individually. But even though we know that one solution does not work for everyone, I can promise you this: If you follow the guidelines in this book and apply them diligently to your situation, you will notice a marked improvement in your relationship with your chosen partner.

Guided by Society

Some members of the upcoming generation may not agree with certain customs and practices in today's society, but they are aware that it is very difficult to ignore them.

One such custom is the practice of marriage. We grow up believing it's best for society if we all get married and live happily ever after. According to an article in *The New York Times*, [9] marriage lengthens life and substantially boosts physical and emotional health. Also, statistics show married couples produce more income than people who are divorced or living together.

From our earliest childhood, most cultures in our society have taught us that when we grow up, getting married is the proper thing to do. Why? Because the interest of society is best served when as many people as possible get married and stay married. Economics is a major factor. People who choose the stability of marriage and family life usually strive to produce more income together, which results in more overall productivity. Also, producing new generations ensures continuation of the society.

So by the time most people become young adults, they have already accepted that one of their major goals is to find a suitable partner so they can continue in the footsteps of their parents and grandparents. They are therefore on a constant lookout for such a person.

If they have not found a marriage partner by a reasonable age, they are pressured by people around them to accelerate the process. Women are usually more anxious than men and more so at an earlier age because, as the saying goes, "their biological clocks may be ticking." This means they may be approaching a stage in their lives when they may no longer be able to produce children because their reproductive system no longer works.

But whether or not people choose to accept their parents' traditions, one thing is certain: Most people are not meant to live their lives alone. Almost everyone (except hermits) needs at least one person with whom to share his or her life. And whether it is marriage or another form of cohabitation, it is reasonable to assume that relationships are here to stay. If traditional concepts of relationships are no longer workable, as we have seen, people must develop new strategies that are more suitable to our changing society.

However, changes do not occur overnight. The lessons learned from our parents (and they from their parents) are well entrenched in our psyches and would take some doing to alter. So in addition to learning the new skills, we also face the task of unlearning what has already been taught. The process is not complicated but it needs effort and dedication if we are to succeed.

Part 1
Choosing the One

Chapter One
Let's start from the beginning

Before you enter into a long-term relationship in which you expect to succeed, you have to be satisfied that you are ready to make a commitment. Put yourself in the other person's shoes. You must be able to look at yourself in the mirror and say, "Yes this is someone I would definitely like to know better." By no means should you begin a relationship from a position of self-doubt, low self-esteem, desperation, or uncertainty. You must decide what you want and know you are capable of achieving your desires. How can you do this?

Whether you are a man or a woman, or you are entering a relationship for the first time, or you have been involved before and would like to try again, become fully aware of who you are and what you want out of life. As you do, you will better be able to understand why you feel the way you do and the reasons for your behavior. With this understanding of yourself, you have the necessary information and freedom to make changes and create the life you want. On the other hand, if you do not know who you are, it would be impossible to make changes if necessary.

What do you want?

In our subconscious mind, most of us know what we truly want, but getting caught up in life's dramas and outside influences causes us to lose sight of our true desires and needs. Sometimes we are uncertain of the true motivation for our actions. Are you asking, "Am I doing this because I want to or because I think I should?"

Now that you are considering a relationship, here's how to identify your wants. Find a quiet place where you can sit by yourself. Make sure that you are not interrupted. Take a few minutes to reflect on your life up to this moment. Think about things you have done (your successes and your failures), and things you enjoy as well as those that were not pleasant. Ask yourself:

- Why do I want a relationship?
- Is it because I am lonely?
- Is it because all my friends are married and I am not?
- Do I feel incomplete without a partner?
- Do I feel that I am growing older and that life may pass me by?

With a pen and a sheet of paper, write down why you feel that you want a relationship. (Note: This is also for people already in a relationship who want to move forward and be more committed.)

Positive reasons for entering a relationship

1. People who are satisfied with their achievements and are happy with who they are usually experience a strong urge to share their lives with someone. If you've seen the movie "Mahogany" starring Diana Ross and Billy D. Williams, you may remember how Billy D made this point clear when Diana Ross was prepared to put everything on the line to become a famous fashion model. He said, "Success means nothing if you don't

have someone you love to share it with." When you feel you possess an abundance of good things in your life, you begin to think, "I can't wait to find my loving equal with whom I can eventually create a family... a family that can benefit from everything I have learned and accomplished."

2. In the company of someone with whom you share true love and intimacy, you can be yourself. You can relax knowing you can confront your strengths and weaknesses, make mistakes, and not be judged adversely.

3. Learning is a continuing process, and a satisfying relationship provides twenty-four hours a day of constant interactive training. There is great hope for success when two people join together in a commitment to experience growth together for them.

Are you ready?

Before you begin your search for a potential partner, be sure of the following:

- That you truly love yourself.
- That you put behind you all past issues and shed all emotional baggage.
- That you're honest in evaluating yourself so you know your strengths and weaknesses.

Loving yourself

Of all the factors vitally important in creating lasting love relationships, I believe self-esteem is the most important. Knowing who you perceive yourself to be and how you feel about yourself are critical when it comes to long-term happiness. Everyone on this earth is here for a reason. Yes, you can always find someone more attractive, better educated or more financially secure than you are, but they can never have the privilege of being you. You possess qualities and attributes many may envy if they get the chance to know the real you. Give them that chance.

People who feel good about themselves radiate a powerful message. They know they are entitled to the best there is to offer and are not prepared to accept any less. This attitude offers a challenge to any prospective relationship candidate you come in contact with. It requires them to put their best foot forward in their dealings with you. Subsequently, they will feel a sense of achievement when they ultimately succeed in living up to your expectations.

Unfortunately, many people find it difficult to accept themselves for who they are. Sometime in their childhood, they acquired the belief that they would have to change many things in their lives if they are to be loved by others. This universal problem has been the cause of great unhappiness for many people.

Remember the old saying, "If we do not love ourselves, we cannot love anyone else." This still holds true, but it is also true that it is almost impossible to believe someone can love us if we do not love ourselves. How many times have we seen relationships suffer because one partner searches for reasons why his or her mate showers love and devotion on him/her? These partners cannot believe they're loved for themselves, they believe they're being deceived and their true motives will come out one of these days. They are convinced they are not worthy of their partner's love.

Dr Nathaniel Branden, in his excellent book *The Psychology of Romantic Love,* explains this phenomenon. He notes that the overwhelming majority of humans suffer from some level of self-esteem deficiency. Deep down in their psyche, they feel unworthy of love. These are not necessarily conscious beliefs. On the surface, it appears they feel entitled to be loved; they may even say "I deserve to be loved." But deep negative feelings lurk in the background, sabotaging their efforts to achieve fulfillment. [10]

The good news is that behavioral therapists have devised methods to assist people in eliminating these deep entrenched psychological beliefs of inferiority. When you love yourself the way you are, you will give yourself permission to act in your own interest. You will not feel guilty for expecting a satisfying relationship because you'll feel that you deserve it. It's almost a self-fulfilling prophecy: When you expect it, it will happen.

Leaving past issues behind

Ending a relationship could be a traumatic experience, and sometimes it seems impossible to recover from the pain. Sooner or later however we have to come to the realization that life goes on and so must we.

There are many painful questions to consider, one of which is "What went wrong?" Finding the answers to this question helps put past issues to rest and prepares the way for a new beginning.

Attempting to start a new relationship without coming to terms with the reasons for the failure of your previous ones presents the following problems:

- You are likely to experience similar problems in a new relationship.
- You will not be emotionally available to commit to a new partner because you will believe you can be hurt again.
- The anger you carry within you will continually work against you, sabotaging every genuine effort you attempt to find new happiness.

Sometimes letting go of past hurt is much more difficult

than expected, because you may not understand the reasons for the problem. This makes you angry and this anger, though not a positive force, keeps you connected to your past relationship.

Consider this scenario. You finally decided to end a relationship because you feel your mate was not giving you what you wanted out of the relationship. The tough part is that he is a wonderful person and you know he truly loves you-at times even more than you love him. The only problem is that sometimes he does certain things he knows are hurtful to you. You say, "I'm sure he knows because I've brought it to his attention many times." Now that he is gone, you cannot stop thinking about him, you cannot understand why he could not be loving to you all the time. It makes you angry because it is clear he had what you needed but refused to give it to you. Why couldn't he? Why didn't he? It is difficult to discard such great memories and becomes even more so when you mentally interact with the kind, caring side of a person you still love.

Yes, it is difficult, but you must be able to shed this anger, resentment, and uncertainty to move on. How do you do this?

First, remember that people are the way they are and it's almost impossible to change them. When you commit to a partner (let's say your partner is male), you are in fact agreeing to accept him with all of his shortcomings. These shortcomings are usually easier to live with in the earlier stages of the relationship because you believe his positive side alone is enough to sustain the relationship. Perhaps his love for you will cause him to change and become more to your liking. However, as time passes, certain flaws in his behavior begin to bother you. Usually these are the same traits, which you ignored at the beginning of the relationship. Yes, you ignored them and now they are back to haunt you. Many times you wonder, "How can someone be so kind at some times and so inconsiderate at other times?" You discuss the matter many times, but the situation does not change.

Understand and accept that at no time your partner intended to hurt you. Even when you felt he was not doing what you believe he should do, he was always doing the best he could. Maybe his upbringing causes him to act in a certain way, or maybe he has certain psychological problems he doesn't understand. So as far as he knows, he is doing OK. You know this because you are certain he loves you and would give you the moon and stars if he could. So take the good with the bad. Your partner has both; the good side was wonderful, the bad side was rotten. You could not accept this so you decided to leave. End of story.

Now you can put this behind you because you understand it's not fair to be angry with your partner. It was not his fault. You cannot, however, deny how wonderful he was and how much he loved you and maybe still does. This part of the relationship you cannot discard. There will always be a place in your heart for good memories. Treasure this love; use it as a reference point for the kind of love you will seek in the future.

Every time you think about your "ex" and focus on your wonderful connection with him, you may feel the urge to return to the relationship, but you don't. You wouldn't because you remember your reasons for leaving and understand that the situation would most likely never change. But now you are free, free from anger and resentment towards your "ex." And now that you have closed this door, you are free to take the steps in creating the satisfying relationship you want and deserve.

Take these steps to get your "ex" out of your mind:

1. Make a clean break.

Once you have made a decision that the relationship is not working, don't waste any more time. Leave immediately. Being with your "ex" has become a habit and you already know that habits are hard to break. So don't call. Don't accept calls. Stick with your decision; you had good reasons for making it. Don't be misled by ego trips. People hate rejection, and even though your "ex" might know there is no good reason for continuing the relationship, he may try to get you back only because you rejected him. Do not fall into this trap.

2. Make a "fault list."

After a break up, most people focus on the good times they spent together with their ex partner. The bad times are often forgotten. Make a complete list of all the mean and unpleasant things your "ex" did to you. Keep this list handy. Whenever you feel nostalgic about returning to your "ex," you can refer to the list.

3. Get back on the horse.

It's difficult to even consider a new relationship immediately after a break up. You must, however, make a special effort to start dating as soon as possible. You may not find someone immediately who fits your ideals. But get out and circulate, meet new people. You don't have to get serious with anyone; casual dating will take your mind off of your "ex." Be very careful. It is so easy to fall for someone when you are in this vulnerable state. If you find yourself feeling closer to someone soon after a break up, make sure you are not mistaken. One way to do this is to stop seeing that person for a while. Go on other dates. If it's "the real thing," you will know.

Shedding emotional beliefs

Many people go through life with unresolved emotional issues. This means that sometime in their lives, perhaps from their childhood, an emotional trauma prevents them from moving forward. In the majority of cases, the people are not consciously aware of their emotional state, causing them to make the same mistakes over and over again.

Most people start out with the best intentions in their relationships. They seem to know what they want and what they must do to reach their goals. They consciously set out to do what they believe is right for them, but somehow end up doing things not in their best interest. For example, you may say, "I know that I need a mate who will be kind and considerate to me," or "I will not date another married man, or anyone else that is not free to commit to me." Yes, you say this, but you end up with a mate who turns out to be abusive or cannot make a serious commitment to you.

Why does this happen? Psychologists have proven conclusively that human behavior is governed by a deep belief system held on a subconscious level. This belief system was acquired in early childhood when we first received important information about life. This information is stored deep in our subconscious minds and represents our "true beliefs." Whatever beliefs we may subsequently acquire usually do not erase our original "true beliefs." So, even when new knowledge and experience guides us to act in a way that seems logical, the subconscious takes over. If what seems logical is different from these *true beliefs*, our actions prove to be different. [11]

Consider people who decide to quit smoking. Every day they read about thousands of people who are suffering from lung cancer and other diseases caused by smoking. They say, "It's insane to continue to sabotage my health. I must stop this. I am going to quit." But within the hour, you see them lighting up another cigarette.

Past traumatic experiences

People who have been betrayed by a close friend or family member, mentally or physically abused by a former mate, or have suffered some other emotional traumas in their lives may find it difficult to trust or commit to anyone again. Sometimes no matter how much we try, we cannot put these unfortunate experiences behind us. In some cases we may not be able to put our finger on the causes of the problem. All we know is that we go into it believing that "this one will work." But we come out saying all men/women are the same: no good, cannot be trusted, selfish, and so on.

If this applies to you, you may be well advised to seek some kind of professional help. There are many qualified professionals who can assist if necessary. Contact your local Chamber of Commerce for more information. Or ask your family doctor to recommend a competent therapist with whom you can privately and confidentially discuss your personal situation.

Know your strengths and weaknesses

Take a good hard honest look at yourself. What have you got to offer a potential partner? Unfortunately, we live in a world where you are judged initially by superficial things. The way you carry yourself, your physical appearance, the value of your home, and your status in the community are all criteria most people use for attractiveness. These superficial attributes may be important for initial attraction, but after this, a person wants to know, "What is he/she really made of?"

So, when considering a new relationship, be realistic in evaluating yourself. How do others see you? Many people believe that, on an eligibility scale of 1 to 10, they rate number 11, then wonder why their phone is not ringing off the hook with date invitations.

There is a great difference between who you are and who you would like to be. Sometimes you can mislead others as to who you really are, especially when meeting for the first time. Usually, it's not your intention to mislead others, but attempting to put your best foot forward can send out mixed signals.

This is one of the principal causes of failure in many relationships. You become attracted to someone because you believe that "what you see is what you get," only to be disappointed later when you get to know the person better.

A good way to truthfully evaluate yourself is to pretend that you are describing yourself to someone. List all of the characteristics you believe best describe you. After you have this list, ask a few close friends to prepare a similar list describing you. You then compare their list with yours. Show your friends your list and ask them individually if they agree with your assessment of yourself. It would be very interesting to hear their assessment of you. Friends are usually not brutally honest, but nevertheless, you will have a good indication of how you are perceived by others.

Questions that determine your eligibility

1. **Are you a person of good character?** It's easy to confuse personality traits with character. Your passion for the finer things in life, your ability to light up the party, your soft touch are attractive personality traits, but your character will determine the success or failure of your relationship. Character is what you are made of, your upbringing, your respect for others, and how you react under stress all indicate your readiness to deal with the multitude of complications inevitable in a relationship.

2. **Do have high integrity.** Knowing that a partner will never willfully lie or mislead you produces a tremendous feeling of security. Honesty and trustworthiness are essential to any successful relationship. When a partner is always honest with you, trust becomes natural. This automatically eliminates many problems that kill relationships, such as, the fear of extramarital affairs. Imagine living in constant fear that your partner may not be truthful with you all the time. You will be in a constant state of nervousness and apprehension. In this state, it is almost impossible to maintain intimacy and passion.

Honesty and integrity is a part of character that does not change easily. Usually when a partner betrays you, you are devastated. You cannot believe someone so close could possibly do such dreadful things. However, if you were to consider the matter carefully, you would realize that a person of high integrity would not normally act in this fashion. You are then faced with the realization that your partner lacked integrity from the beginning.

3. Are you committed to personal growth? Someone who is ready and willing to learn as much as he/she can about themselves with the intention of making improvements where possible is a good candidate for a successful relationship. Such commitment to personal growth and improvement guarantees a better relationship because it avoids some of the primary causes of failure in a love union between two people. An example is power struggles, when two people fight desperately to prove that one is right and the other is wrong. Sometimes one partner can see the need for improvement while the other stays in denial.

You need a mate who knows that every relationship experiences rough spots and is ready to work with you to find solutions when faced with a problem. Before you commit to someone, it is important to determine how committed he/she is to self-improvement. Many people fail to determine this at the beginning, only to find out in a time of crisis that their partner is too stubborn to read a book on relationships, listen to self-development tapes, or seek professional assistance. Commitment to personal growth and improvement is probably the single most important ingredient in a relationship. If either you or your partner lacks this commitment, it is very unlikely your relationship will survive.

4. Are you a mature and responsible person? Let's face it, not everyone is ready to enter a committed relationship. You may possess many great qualities as a person and be capable of loving someone, but you need a certain level of maturity to sustain a lasting relationship. Maturity in this case does not refer to age. Many women tell me they always seek older men because they are usually more mature. This may be true in some cases, but the high number of unsuccessful second and third marriages proves that age alone does not guarantee maturity. A mature person is grown up enough to know that each individual and no one else is responsible for his or her own life. Each person must be able to:

- Provide the necessary financial resources to support themselves.
- Be conscious of and able to maintain good health habits.
- Be able to feed themselves, which includes being able to prepare their own meals if necessary.

This does not mean you cannot seek assistance or share responsibilities, but the ultimate accountability is yours. One of the reasons parents do not put a large burden of responsibility on children is because they are not mature enough to accept it. Mature adults, on the other hand are expected to exhibit some form of responsibility, meaning, they do what they say they will do. They are accountable for their actions and decisions, regardless of the consequences.

It is easy to determine if someone is responsible. A person who is always late for appointments, always has a good excuse for being out of a job, or always needs to be taken care of by someone is not ready to accept responsibility. Such a person may be nice to have as a casual friend, but may prove difficult to live with as a love partner.

One characteristic that identifies a successful relationship is the feeling of security experienced by both partners. This kind of security comes with knowing you can count on your partner's support in a time of need. It is refreshing to find someone with whom you can share all the wonderful things life has to offer and who has the same enthusiasm as you. You also want someone who stands by your side in a time of emergency, during illness, and through stressful situations.

Most people who possess the characteristics mentioned above are in high demand in the world of relationships. Many refer to them as prime marriage/relationship material.

If you can answer yes to the four categories of questions listed above, you can place yourself high on the scale of eligibility for lifelong relationships.

Eligible but still single

Joanne is a 33-year-old pharmacist who has never been married. "Where did all the good guys go?" she asks. "I have been dating men for the past three years and still can't find one whom I consider worthwhile. My friends suggest I may be setting my standards too high and perhaps I should consider compromising. But most of the men I meet do not even come close to what I am looking for. I feel I have a lot to offer to the right man, if only I can find him."

I have interviewed many young women who find themselves in a similar situation. These women have chosen to pursue careers instead of opting for early marriage and perhaps motherhood. These women have achieved economic and personal independence; they are now in a position to exercise some measure of control over their lives. They feel ready to find an equal partner with whom they can share their lives.

These women say that finding a man who meets their criteria has not been easy. However, at a closer look, the situation for these women may be even more complicated than it might appear.

Finding an equal

Modern women continue to speak out against what they see as male domination resulting from an uneven role balance between the partners in a relationship. They are no longer prepared to accept the role of a traditional wife. So they seek a mate with whom they can share an equal partnership. But here's the problem. While growing up, many women heard these words from their mothers: "Never marry a man you cannot look up to." That refers to a man who is more than an equal; perhaps more intelligent, more ambitious, and more socially established.

So even though a woman may truly want to find an equal, her lifelong training and her need to be socially accepted influences her selection. She may hold out for the kind of man that would meet her mother's approval. Of course, some women get tired of waiting and select a man of their own choice. This works out fine for many women, but others may go through a period of torment by guilt for what they see as letting their mothers down.

However, if the woman chooses to hold out for her ideal man, i.e., the one she could look up to, she may remain single for a long period. Why? Because most men who fit such profiles fall into a few categories and are usually in short supply. For example, let's refer to him as type 'A'; a well adjusted, self-confident, and progressive man who actually wants an equal love partner. Such a man may not feel comfortable in a relationship in which his woman believes she has to look up to him. Unbelievable as it may seem, such men do exist but are not easy to find.

Then there is Type 'B'; the man who feels he has earned the right to have a beautiful woman at his side, a trophy wife. This is the type that some societies label "a good catch" and who himself believes he is God's special gift to women. Such a man would probably run in the opposite direction when he encounters an ambitious and independent woman who demonstrates she is clearly in control of her life.

Women who have been able to side-step the traditional rules and successfully chart their own destiny should congratulate themselves. They have indeed earned the right to be picky when it comes to selecting the person with whom to share their lives.

The time has come to reinvent new standards for relationships, standards that will be more suitable to the needs of a new generation. The traditional concepts of relationships have served their purpose, but are now outdated even though society still clings to them. Imagine our parents may still believe that a man who does not have a regular job is not a good catch for their daughter. Most people know that many other avenues exist today and one can achieve economic stability without having a steady job.

In the 1991 hit movie "Father of the Bride," Steve Martin who played the father became disturbed when he learned that Annie his daughter (Kimberly Williams) was about to marry Bryan (George Newbern), an independent communications consultant. Even when Annie explained that her fiancée gets contracts with various companies, he was still not impressed. Why didn't Bryan have a permanent job? Only after Annie explained that Bryan was such a high-priced consultant that no one company could afford to keep him on their permanent staff was her father relieved.

Old customs and traditions die hard. But the time has come when we have to find ways of shedding old beliefs and setting new standards that meet current individual needs. The beliefs of the older generation have served them well. However, what was right for them may not be right for generations that follow. It's necessary to create new rules to solve the new problems of today.

You, more than anyone else, must know if someone is right for you. Ignore the fantasies and old fairy tales; create new ones that suit you better. Instead of waiting to be swept off your feet, keep your feet firmly planted on the ground.

Chapter Two
Developing a plan

It is a common belief that romance is a natural process; it will happen if you just allow nature to take its course. You may be familiar with popular comments like, "Marriages are made in heaven," or "I will know it when the right person comes along." Even if you believe these to be true, it would not hurt the process to develop strategies to give Mother Nature a helping hand. Most successful people do not wait for things to happen; they make them happen. Developing a plan transforms your dreams into reality. You know what you want, and a plan gives you the necessary tools and direction to accomplish your goals.

Where do you begin?

1. Visualize. You have heard this before: Everything starts with a dream. In the absence of dreams, very little seems to happen. There is, however, a great difference between dreaming and visualizing. You need to know where you're going before beginning your journey, so you'll want to "see" a clear picture of yourself succeeding. The Oxford English definition of "visualize" is: "To bring something as a picture before the mind." When you can see it, you will believe it can happen to you!

Picture yourself after a rough day relaxing in the comfort of your home with a partner whom you truly love and respect, a friend with whom you can comfortably discuss your innermost feelings and know you will be supported. Imagine… that after several years together, you still feel the same passion for your lover that you felt at the beginning of your love affair. Imagine... that after all this time, you can look your partner in the eyes and say "I like you." Paint a picture of yourself in the future; visualize exactly where you would like to be, and then take the necessary steps to get there.

2. Write it down. Once you've decided on your goals and your plan of action, write it down. Many people believe this is a waste of time, but writing down your goals and your plan of action provides you with a road map to guide you. Remember, if your goals are not written down, they are not goals but only dreams, and we know that dreams take a longer time to come true.

In his book Unlimited Power, Anthony Robbins refers to a study of the 1953 Graduates of Yale University. The graduates were asked if they had a clear specific set of goals and a plan for achieving them, and if they were written down. Only three percent had written down their goals! When the members of the graduating class of 1953 were interviewed 20 years later, the three percent of graduates who had written goals were more financially successful than the other 97 percent put together. It was also significant to note that apart from financial success, the interviewers determined that the same three percent enjoyed happier and more contented lives. [12]

3. Be Specific. When setting goals, be specific. Say exactly what you want to achieve. Your brain works like a camera; it takes a picture of your goals and stores it. Being specific eliminates confusion, so instead of saying, for example, "I want a mate who would be ideal for me," say, "I want a mate who is honest and trustworthy, independent, responsible, kind and loving to me, and is ready for a lasting relationship." Your brain then records this information in its archives and serves as a reminder every step of the way. Whenever you encounter difficulties and are tempted to quit, a mental picture surfaces to remind you of the reasons for your efforts.

Here are some items to include in your action plan list:

- Notify close friends and relatives of my intentions.
- Join clubs and interest groups.
- Engage in healthy activities, e.g., enroll in a health club, and eat healthy foods.
- Accept more invitations to parties and social functions.
- Go out on dates.

4. Take one step at a time. Keep in mind several steps you need to be successful when seeking a lasting love relationship. For example, what do you do after the dating process? Recommended steps will be covered later in this book; however, the entire process must be clear in your mind before you begin your journey. Be sure to complete each step before you embark on the next one.

Your ultimate goal is a combination of several intermediate smaller goals. Bypassing even one small target could seriously affect reaching your desired outcome. This phenomenon is true for almost every goal you set in life, but it is especially crucial when your ultimate goal is to find the relationship that is right for you. For example, you may neglect to ask a relevant question or confirm important data about a prospective mate. Subsequently you discover (always too late) certain facts about your partner that you simply cannot live with. Usually this information could have been obtained by asking the pertinent questions before making a final commitment. This could have avoided a situation that does not serve your best interests.

5. Review your progress regularly. Failure is not a sudden event; it does not happen overnight. If you retraced your steps whenever failure occurs, you can usually identify a series of errors and poor decisions, which were responsible for such failure. More often than not, these errors in judgment were repeated over and over again, so it's easy to understand why subsequent failure was inevitable.

You can avoid repeating the same mistakes by taking stock of your actions to determine if you are heading in the right direction.

You may say, "Ok, I set my goals and followed my plan, but after three months I have not found anyone. What do I do next?" Whatever you do, **do not give up**. Like every important project, finding a suitable mate requires time. Maybe you have not come in contact with the right people; maybe you are not going to the right places. Stop and review your plan, analyze your strategy. Think about ways you can make some changes (e.g., join a different interest group, change your venues for meeting people.) Remember, every roadblock in your journey helps in the learning process. It provides new data you can use to improve your strategy. Whenever you encounter difficulty or disappointment, consider these as opportunities and not as setbacks. Analyze new information, modify your plan accordingly, and proceed with confidence knowing you are better equipped to reach your target.

Finding your ideal love partner

Now that you have completed all the preliminary steps, you are ready to embark on your search for your ideal love partner. The search for an ideal mate in itself can prove to be an exciting, enjoyable, and enlightening experience. Visiting new places, meeting new people, dining and dancing, and so on, can put new hope into your life.

Casual dating activities

A good way to begin this process is by casual dating. That's when you don't expect everyone you go out with is a potential candidate for a relationship. Your goal here is to meet and learn about as many people as you can, and have fun while doing so.

People who have recently ended a relationship, have been out of the dating scene for some time, or are simply fed up with their limited opportunities to meet new people could find the prospect of casual dating satisfying.

Here's what happens when you decide to date casually:

1. You find out whom you attract and whom you are attracted to.

When you make yourself available for dating, you will be approached by a variety of interested candidates. Here you can learn what kinds of people find you attractive. If you are a woman, you may notice you are attracting men seeking casual affairs. Since this is not the type of relationship you are seeking, you may want to take stock of yourself and determine why you attract this type of person. Perhaps it's the way you dress, the signals you send, or the places you frequent. If, for example, you spend a lot of time at singles' bars, you may give the impression you are only out to have a good time. If you don't like the results, you are getting, modify your activities to fit the ones you seek.

David, 35, a businessman known to be financially successful, says, "I find it difficult to find a woman I can take seriously. I want to have a genuine love relationship, but even when I carefully select someone, I discover that most of my dates are primarily interested in material things."

This problem is common among men who are famous, physically well endowed, or financially successful. Many seldom get the chance to select a truly compatible mate because women who seek these qualities in men constantly bombard them. The truth is that most of these women are themselves attractive, confident, aggressive, and accessible, hence irresistible to most men. So it should come as no surprise that such eligible men always find themselves in the company of these attractive women.

2. You will feel wanted.

Every time someone asks you for a date, it reinforces your self-esteem so if you have been out of the dating scene for some time, you may feel unwanted or undesirable. After you begin to go out on as many dates as possible, you will find that many people will approach you. You may even find it difficult to fit all of your activities into your schedule. Such activities could greatly change your outlook about yourself and your views about the opposite sex. Perhaps you felt responsible for the failures in your last relationships; maybe you thought you were not good enough. Now you find you get along well with many people; you have even received a few serious proposals. When you feel good about yourself, it puts sparkle in your life, making you more attractive to a prospective partner.

3. You will form new relationships.

Casual dating is a good way to meet new people. Someone you date can introduce you to acquaintances that may share similar interests as yourself. This could lead to forming many new relationships and ultimately to creating the ideal relationship you want.

4. You get comfortable and eliminate your inhibitions.

Some people are genuinely shy and will not expose themselves to the opposite sex for fear of rejection. After you have been on several dates, you gain the confidence to be yourself. You feel comfortable enough to sit back and observe people. You can objectively look at someone and decide whether he or she possesses the qualities you expect in a mate. In the arena of casual dating, you will also learn more about yourself; why you react a certain way in the presence of some people, how you behave on a first date, and what is your reaction when you feel attracted to someone.

As you get more comfortable, you will be able to set standards and boundaries. You will learn to eliminate the people you feel are not suitable for you. When you date a lot, you can practice setting boundaries. This means you can firmly but gently let people know what you will and will not accept. The respect you gain from setting boundaries goes a long way to improving your self-image.

Chapter Three
Your game plan for dating

For many, dating is a painful exercise, so it is no surprise that some people go about their lives simply hoping that Mr. or Ms. Right will show up when the time is right. The result is that many people remain single and unattached much longer than they need to be.

This chapter provides you with guidelines to help eliminate stress so dating will be an enjoyable experience. One way to ensure you will find a suitable mate is to date as many prospects as you physically can. Yes, I know that could be time consuming so you wonder, "How do I fit all this in my already overloaded schedule?"

The answer is you maintain a dating diary. This way, you can keep track of all your activities, record valuable information about your dates, and make efficient use of your time. I'm not suggesting you sit in a restaurant making notes as you speak. But mentally record your conversations and make notes as soon as you return home. Complete this exercise as soon as possible while the details are fresh in your mind. Otherwise you could forget valuable information.

People who are basically shy or apprehensive about venturing out on the dating scene may discover that proper organization of activities could eliminate dating phobia. Imagine skillfully organizing your week to include new activities, declining date invitations that cannot fit in your schedule, and eliminating prospects whom do not meet your initial requirements. Maintaining a busy calendar helps build your self-confidence, which can assist in changing your outlook of the dating world. And remember, dating should at all times be enjoyable.

Where do you find eligible prospects?

Although certain places may have a higher ratio of singles than others, unattached people can be found everywhere. Many singles in search of a suitable partner overlook some of the most obvious places. The building complex where you live, your neighborhood supermarket or laundromat, the local coffee shop or deli counter are all places where you can make new friends.

The most important thing is your attitude. A woman with a friendly face and a cool disposition will always attract conversations from men. If you are a man, do not hesitate to start a friendly conversation with the woman beside you; you may be pleasantly surprised at the reception you get. Look for hints; a woman buying pet food would most likely have a pet. Observe; the items in her cart should give you an idea whether she is single. I myself have walked up to women in a Macys and asked, "Excuse me. I've been trying to find some accessories to match the colors in my living room. Do you have any suggestions? I've found this to be a good way to start a conversation.

Other activities you can do by yourself:

- Take walks. It keeps you in shape and may lead to meeting someone. If you have a pet take it along with you.
- Go window-shopping in malls. You don't have to buy anything, but you will sure see a lot of people.

- Go bike riding.
- Enroll in a dance class. Choose the type of dance you enjoy. It doesn't have to be a six-month course; a few classes would be fun and puts you with others who enjoy dancing.
- Do volunteer work. If you don't know where to begin, contact your local chamber of commerce. It offers hundreds of activities requiring volunteers. Engage in activities you enjoy or else you may get bored and quit.
- Attend trade shows. Here you will have an opportunity to learn new ideas, broaden your areas of interests, and expand your circle of acquaintances.
- If you're retired, look for a part time job. It doesn't have to be anything strenuous or time consuming, but it's something that keeps you in contact with people.
- Go to bookstores. Modern bookstores are designed with readers comfort in mind. You can sit for hours reading your favorite books. Many have coffee shops where you can drink and eat while reading.
- Visit hardware stores and do-it-yourself shops, to find someone who might share your interest in home improvement.
- Join a health club.
- Go to auto races.

You don't need a partner for these activities and all of them provide excellent opportunities to meet new friends. Remember, always wear a pleasant smile and do the things, you enjoy most.

Introductions through friends

Let your close friends know you are in the market for a mate. Most friends (especially those already in a relationship) are happy to assist you in finding your significant other. Get out your old phonebook and call everyone you know. Find out how they are doing and make arrangements to get together with them. The more you stay in contact, the more chances you have of being invited to functions where you can meet new people.

You will likely feel more comfortable with introductions from friends because true friends want the best for you. It may be helpful, however, to indicate your preferences so you avoid any waste of time. Let it be known, for example, that you have no interest in a mate who has been married before and has children, or someone whose job involves constant travel.

If a referral from a friend works out, you should let your friends know you had a good time and you appreciate their assistance. It is not wise to give details to your friends about your new relationship, especially if you feel that it can go further. Remember, when you date a friend of a friend, you have to work harder to maintain your privacy.

You'll find it tempting to discuss intimate information about your newfound mate with your mutual friend. Maybe you would like to (a) share your good fortune in finding someone you are happy with, and (b) want to obtain more information to assist you in furthering your new relationship. Resist this urge; it could backfire in your face. Always remember that information reported to a mutual friend will be repeated to your newfound lover, and this could have unpleasant consequences.

Bars and nightclubs

Self-proclaimed experts in the field of dating and relationships say that bars and nightclubs are among the worst places to meet prospects for a lasting relationship. It's because people who frequent such places usually just want to have a good time.

Even if this is true, you can still make periodic visits for the purpose of socializing. The fact is that such venues provide a way for singles to congregate, and you can make new contacts and possibly develop new friendships.

Janet, age 36, used to visit a different bar on her way home from work at least once a week. She would order a non-alcoholic beverage, sit with her notepad, and review the events of her day. She always seemed to be involved in what she was doing, paying no attention to the men that surrounded her.

Almost on every occasion, a man would approach her with the intention of starting a conversation. If the man seemed OK, she would accept his company. If not, she would smile and say, "I'm trying to finish something at this moment, maybe later." Janet met and selected numerous dates in this fashion. She has been happily married for eight years to a man she refers to as the sweetest person she has ever met. And she met him at a bar!

Most men do not expect their wives to be frequent patrons of bars and nightclubs, and they are less likely to marry women they meet under such circumstances. You should know, however, that exceptions exist. For example, certain ethnic groups have a more positive attitude towards bars than others. The type and location of the bar or nightclub also makes a difference; a sophisticated bar in midtown Manhattan or Toronto would be more acceptable than a local tavern in Queens or Brooklyn.

You could even be one of those people who finds meaningful acquaintances in bars. Here are a few suggestions to follow.

For women:

1. Do not allocate a large chunk of your time to bars. Spend about two to three hours in the early evening, preferably during weekdays. Many businessmen and office workers stop at a nearby bar on their way home. During this time, you can make acquaintances with people and plan further meetings. At no time should you turn a casual meeting at a bar into a date, because you risk giving the impression you casually pick up dates at bars.

2. Sit by yourself. Even if you need a ride from friends, split up before you enter. You can regroup later when you are ready to leave. If you sit in the company of friends (whether it be men or women), men would find it difficult to approach you. Why? Because they may think that you are connected to one of the men in your group, or they might be too timid to intrude.

3. Maintain a constant state of alertness. Depending on your tolerance, consume little or no alcohol. This means you can sip a glass of wine to be social. If you accept another drink from someone before you finish the previous one, discard the previous drink and continue to sip on the new one. If you are thirsty, quench your thirst with a glass of water or a non-alcoholic beverage. This is important to keep in mind, because it's easy to consume more alcohol than you planned and may lose control.

4. Don't get stuck with an undesirable. You do not want to appear to be snobbish, but you cannot afford to waste your time on someone with whom you feel uncomfortable. If a man asks to join you, do not accept drinks from him until you are satisfied you can tolerate his company. Some people appear to be normal at first, but they can become unbearable while in your company. Maybe they have drunk too much or maybe they are simply jerks. Whatever the reason, you need to distance yourself from them as quickly as you can. You can do this gracefully by asking for an excuse. "I've just spotted a group of friends, I'll be going to join them," or "Excuse me I must go powder my nose." Take your belongings, handbag, drink, keys, etc., so you would have no reason to return.

5. A word of caution. If at any time you have to leave your table, finish what you're drinking. When you return, order a fresh drink. At no time you should drink from a glass that has been out of your sight, even for a minute. You may have heard horror stories of people who have fallen victims to others with malicious intentions. The reports are numerous where substances commonly known as date rape drugs have been placed in the drinks of unsuspecting victims in bars and nightclubs. The victims are usually taken to a different location where they are abused. Don't believe for a moment this applies to women only. I have read stories where men have awakened to find their apartments ransacked and their belongings stolen by women they dated.

For men:

1. Go easy on the alcohol. Many women say they avoid going to bars because they feel uncomfortable and even terrified by men who have had too much to drink. Women find it difficult to take men seriously if they are under the influence of alcohol.

2. Do not give up until you meet someone you like. Ask a woman to dance or introduce yourself and ask if you can join her for some conversation. If you are turned down, go to the other side of the bar and try again. Do not stop until you find someone who accepts your invitation. Most men are devastated after their first few rejections so they rush back to the bar and order a double.

Be aware that a rejection might not have anything to do with you. Perhaps she has just entered the bar and would like to relax before engaging in conversation, or perhaps she might be expecting a friend to join her.

Some guys find it better to engage in a short conversation with the woman, even if she refuses their company. They say, "Ok, it seems like you are expecting someone. If you feel like some company later, I'll be right over there. Maybe I can offer you something to drink in the meantime." This kind of conversation could go on for two or three minutes and seems to be better than immediately turning and walking away after a rejection.

Matchmaking

Formal matchmaking has become sophisticated in recent times. Today, matchmaking professionals would most likely be referred to as relationship consultants. People operating these services usually have backgrounds in behavioral sciences with extensive experience in relationship counseling.

Some services employ computer and Internet technology to bring couples together. They tap into powerful matching software to access databases and use them to locate profiles of members that match the criteria you specify, e.g., age, geographic area, religion, children, etc. If you select someone and someone selects you, you are then given email addresses so you can communicate at your convenience.

Most matchmaking services have the following in common:

1. Their clients are made up of busy professionals and career men and women who have little time or opportunity to meet new people.

2. Clients are limited to a specific number of introductions within a year, but it is highly likely that you will find someone compatible. The people you meet through matchmaking, like yourself, have made a sizable monetary investment in their love lives. They are extremely serious about finding a suitable mate.

3. The cost of matchmaking services can be expensive, e.g., $1500 for six dates. But like everything else, you get what you pay for. If a proposed match does not fit, both parties are asked to fill out questionnaires and explain why the match was not suitable. The matchmaker then evaluates the information to assess what is necessary for a perfect match.

Some services provide counseling as part of the package. A counselor would schedule several sessions with a member to better prepare him/her to find a suitable companion.

Of course, you need to shop around because the quality of service may vary widely. You must take into consideration that a new company will have a limited number of members. Also, be aware that the majority of small businesses fail within the first year. So before you pull out your check book, make sure you obtain the following information:

- How long has the company been in operation?
- What is the ratio of men to woman in the age group you are seeking? You may find that in your preference group, the selection may be limited.
- What is the geographic location of members in your preference group? This is particularly important today, especially with online services. Many services promote that they are countrywide, but what good it is to you if most of the eligible prospects live in San Francisco while you live in New York.

Advertising for a mate

Placing ads for a companion in the Personals has become popular today, yet many people still express negative feelings toward this practice. Some say that mostly weirdos, kinky people, and desperately lonely folks place these ads. The question that always comes to mind when discussing this topic is: "Does it really work? And how safe is it?"

Then there are many who are tired of being assessed for their money, social status, etc. These people welcome the opportunity to be able to communicate with strangers who can assess them for who they really are and not what they have. Imagine being in the position of a man who can never be sure if a woman finds him attractive because he is rich or because he is a likable person.

The Personals provide a central location for people who may never otherwise come into contact with each other. But, like everything else, you have to exercise caution. Remember, you have no way of knowing if anything written in a personal ad is true. Many people seek to take advantage of another's needs for companionship.

They tell you exactly what you want to hear so as to gain your confidence. But whatever they tell you over the telephone or via the Internet, you must always keep in mind it takes time and reinforcing behavior for you to learn about a person. Anyone can be on his or her best behavior for a few dates until that drug abuse problem or that violent behavior surfaces.

Deborah is a legal assistant in a Chicago law office. She talks about her experience with Personals, saying, "I was beginning to think that something was wrong with me. After dating several men, I still was unable to find anyone even close to what I was looking for. A friend of mine suggested I place an ad in the newspaper. Like many other women, I felt embarrassed to advertise for a mate, so I declined. I decided, however, to scan the personal sections in various newspapers. I was surprised to find that many of the people advertising were professionals, career women and men. It was then I decided to give it a try, especially since it was anonymous. You can imagine my surprise only a week after my ad was published when I received 60 replies. I had to reorganize my schedule to be able to communicate with all of the prospects. I prepared an information sheet on each one who seemed OK; Of course, there were some undesirables, whom I eliminated immediately. I narrowed my list to 25. I then proceeded to call every one of them and set up appointments to meet in a nearby coffee shop. It was difficult to eliminate more than 10 of the selected 25, because most of them were desirable in one way or another. It took me about six months to go out on dates with 13 of the prospects who answered my ad. This was probably due to the fact that I went on two and three dates with some of them. I am now happily married to one of the men I met through the Personals. It does a lot for your self-confidence when you have a list of eligible prospects to choose from. My experience with the Personals has taught me there are many eligible people, who also need a mate."

Ads force you to clarify your preferences in a mate.

Most advertising media set charges according to space used; some even limit copy to a specified number of words. Therefore, you have to be specific when describing the partner you are seeking.

You may be surprised at the number of people who are not fully conscious about what they would and would not accept in a mate. It is best to set limits and not go beyond them under any circumstances. Some people refer to these limits as **non-negotiable** needs.

So when you compose an ad, you come face to face with specifying exactly what you want in as few words as possible. Sometimes a woman may not want to admit to friends that a mate's height, physical build, facial features, and skin color are important to her. She may casually say that nice people come in all shapes, sizes and colors. But her ad may look somewhat like this.

"...If you are attractive, 5'11 or taller, please send photo to..."

The content of your ad makes a difference.

At all times, accentuate your positive points. If, for instance, you are witty person, let it show by writing a funny ad. You may have a special hobby or career so you write, "Like to spend weekends racing my Kawasaki 1100 cc motorcycle." "Speak two foreign languages and enjoy traveling to foreign countries," "Sipping espresso while listening to an outdoor band at Rockefeller Center is my idea of a good time."

Doreen has met many new friends in the Personals. She says, "I was surprised to learn how many men were interested in dating a woman fire fighter. At first I did not want to mention my profession in the ad, but from the responses I received, I'm glad I did."

Remember, advertising is a competitive business; the ad that receives the most attention will get the most responses.

Do not appear desperate or too serious. Don't write something like, "Looking for someone to embark on a meaningful relationship, maybe get married, and have kids." You may scare someone who genuinely intends to marry and have kids some day. These matters are better dealt with after you get to know each other.

Don't look for sympathy. Stories about terminating a bad relationship, being between jobs, and being tired of the dating scene are unattractive. People may sympathize with you once they get to know you, but bombarding them with your problems beforehand sends negative signals.

Don't lie. Remember, you are looking for someone who will accept you for who you are. You cannot afford to waste time on people who respond to your ad believing you are something you're not. You may be afraid to reveal your weight, height, or general appearance, thinking you may be too fat, too short, or too unattractive. But the reality is that for every size, shape, and interest, someone out there has that preference. Some men prefer heavier women to slim ones. Others prefer a plain Jane who is more likely to appreciate their love to a glamorous woman who feels she has numerous options.

Although both men and women respond to personal ads, it seems men are more likely than women to answer an ad, according to information obtained from matchmaking services. This is not to say that men cannot benefit from placing ads, also.

Responding to an ad puts a woman in the disadvantageous position of being in competition with many other women interested in meeting the same man.

So by all means try the Personals. Remember that an ad that is short, upbeat, funny, flirtatious, and creative will generate the most positive responses.

Men seeking foreign brides

More North American men are turning to countries outside of their own in the search for love than in the past. At a first glance, one might see this practice as an outlet for older North American men seeking younger women. Indeed this may be true in some cases, but the hundreds of international matchmaking services that have sprung up in recent years may tell a different story. It would seem from that many men in their 20s and 30s are turning to other countries in search of something they believe may be lacking in American women. [13]

Contrary to some popular misconceptions, men who seek foreign wives are not doing so because they want women who are submissive and would be ready to do their bidding. These men are seeking women whose attitudes toward marriage is like those of their parents and grandparents. They want the kind of women whose orientation is more toward being a wife than pursuing a career. This is not to say their women cannot have careers; it means they are wives and family caretakers first and career women second.

Most North American women may not meet this criteria, but many men marry them anyway hoping they will change and become closer to what the men want. The outcome of this hopefulness is well known. The result is an army of divorced, separated, and never married men who are unable to find what they want among North American women. These men are not all unattractive or over-the-hill losers as some people may believe. Most are eligible men who want what most men have always wanted. That is:

- Women who are attracted to them and need them as men.
- Women who have strong family values and are prepared to make sacrifices necessary to create and nurture their offspring.
- Women who appreciate and value traditional attributes in a man such as commitment, stability and security, honesty, integrity, and love.

According to Gary Clark author of the book *Your Bride is in the Mail,* It is also a myth that "Foreign Brides" are limited to desperate women in poorer countries whose only goal is to live in North America. There are a few of those, but the majority of women who eventually marry North American men are well educated, socially skilled, and, for the most part, physically attractive. [14]

Of course, the opportunity to emigrate to North America can be enticing to people in less developed countries, but most foreign women who use international referral services are seeking a mate whose attitudes toward women are different to the attitudes of the men at home. In many countries, North American men have a reputation of being faithful, loyal, and considerate husbands. In some Latin American countries, men are known to run around on their wives and take pride in being referred to as Casanovas. For the women who are family oriented (and these are in the majority in such countries), a North American is an excellent alternative. [15]

Best of both worlds

I met two mining engineers who worked for a well-known Canadian mining conglomerate in Venezuela. They were contracted to remain in Venezuela for a period of one year. During that time they dated Venezuelan women and both were talking about divorcing their Canadian wives. One of the guys, Brad, 43, admitted this was the first time in his life he had experienced true love. "Never in my life have I been treated with so much love and attention by any woman, even before and during my present marriage. These women sure know how to treat a man."

Brad extended his stay in Venezuela for another year and when I saw him during that time, he had already started divorce proceedings with his wife.

Many North American men who have had dealings with women from other countries, especially those in Latin America, express similar feelings for the way these women treat them. It may be due to the limited availability of "good men" at home or the fact that people still live by the old rules. Whatever the reasons, it provides a great opportunity for North American males who choose foreign women to enjoy the best of both worlds because:

- They can find a wife who is just as physically attractive as most beautiful North American women.
- Most of these women seem to know how to please a man the old-fashioned way.
- They are happy to cook, clean, and take care of their families the way men remembered their grandmothers did.
- Most of them are educated, socially prepared enough, and willing to enter the work force if necessary.

If, however, the man chooses to take an active part in raising his family, a foreign wife will more than likely welcome his involvement since she already knows and appreciates the importance of joint parenting in raising a family.

But do these marriages last? According to a U.S. Census report, the number of marriages resulting from international dating services is relatively small. Only .021 percent of the women marry men from the U.S. However, a report from the Commission on Filipinos Overseas and information obtained from some international agencies states that marriages arranged through these services tend to have a lower divorce rate than the national average. Eighty percent of these marriages have lasted a number of years. [16]

Using international matchmaking services

As with other forms of prospecting for love, men who seek mates on the international market should proceed with caution. (I say men because there is no real demand for North American women interested in finding a foreign husband; I have not seen a single international singles ad promoting nor advertising for North American women.)

There are many international matchmaking services advertised in newspapers, magazines, and on the Internet, but you have to be selective. Find out exactly what services are being offered before you engage an agency. Some of these companies are more focused on selling trips and tours rather than finding suitable women for their clients. Get references from people who have used the services if you can.

As with other methods of searching for a mate already mentioned in this book, seeking a bride on the international market ought not to be undertaken hastily. And according to Gary Clark, author of *Your Bride is in the Mail*, two way communications by letter writing is probably a good place to begin. "Lengthy two-way communications is most likely to result in a lasting marriage because it is a filtering process that demands up-front work, effort, and dedication on both sides. It thus tends to be biased against those who are less dedicated to finding a compatible mate. Since it is done blind and at a distance, there is less motivation on either side to be false. The opportunity is there to ask probing questions of a large number of prospects. Neither side has made any great investment in the other at that point. It is a PROCESS that lends itself more towards genuineness and honesty than other processes," says Clark.

However, today many international matchmaking services offer to instantly connect you to your dream bride. Today, you can step off the plane in Russia or elsewhere and be whisked away to a social gathering where you can meet a variety of eligible women for the choosing. You are even provided with a language translator if you need one. Some men have been known to fall in love on the spot and subsequently marry women they have met on one of these trips.

When you find someone you feel can be right for you, take time to learn more about her before you make a final decision to marry. Check out her family background, and lifestyle in her own country. Meet some of her friends. These are some of the things you should do prior to making wedding plans. It is easy to misinterpret behavioral traits and customs in people whose culture is different from your own. For example, people who speak a foreign language may express themselves so aggressively that you may get the impression that they are annoyed, when in fact they are engaged in a friendly conversation.

Beware of scams

The majority of women who advertise themselves as eligible brides do so with one intention: to find a North American or other Western husband. However, there have been several instances of serious misrepresentation. I am not referring to lying about age and social standing, or even altering photographs to enhance their looks. Indeed, there are many such cases. (And of course the man will have to decide whether or not he can in fact marry a woman after he finds out she has been untruthful.) However, there are both professional and petit con artists who use pen pal agency services to prey on unsuspecting, naive American men.

As with most scams, the intentions of the perpetrators are to extract money from their victims. At first glance, many North Americans do not recognize these schemes as scams because, in many cases, the amount of money requested is usually insignificant. An example is the foreign currency Collection scams. It works like this: After a few letters of correspondence, the woman asks her North American pen pal to send her a few small bills to add to her currency collection. More than likely, the man does not see this as a big deal, and to make a good impression he may send a 5, 10 and maybe even a 20 dollar bill. Now you can see how a dedicated individual who writes 500 letters a month can enjoy a lucrative enterprise even by North American standards.

Tips on avoiding scams

Though these may seem to be small amounts of money you don't want to waste your time with undesirables. Rules for dealing with foreign women:

- Do not send money.
- Be wary of statements such as:
- Send me money for airfare to visit you.
- Send me money to secure your hotel when you come to visit me.

- My mother needs an operation and I don't have the money.
- She's in love with you the moment she saw your picture.

And don't be surprised if, after several letters of correspondence, you discover your intended pen pal bride turns out to be a man.

You can learn everything you need to know about international dating by visiting Gary Clark's website at: http://www.wtw.org/mob/

If you are interested in Russian women First Dream.com is the place to start. Jack Bragg of First Dream has assisted many men in finding their dream bride. He has also compiled a list with pictures of known and suspected scammers. Jack claims that the information posted on his website has helped more than 100 men who, by their own admissions might have otherwise fallen into the hands of seasoned scammers. Check out his website and his "Hall of Shame" at http://www.firstdream.com

CHAPTER FOUR
Dating

Now that you have a variety of avenues to meet people, you can begin dating. Whatever you may have believed about a prospect, you can make a proper evaluation only after a face-to-face meeting.

Dating provides an opportunity to meet and develop relationships. It gives you the chance to evaluate a variety of prospects and, at the same time, allows them to learn about you.

With all these changes in your new social life, you can find yourself overwhelmed with activity. The only way to maintain control over the situation is to get organized, so invest in a good day planner and use it.

A good way to proceed when meeting a stranger for the first time is to arrange a mini date. This shorter version of a standard date gives you the chance to make a quick initial evaluation of a person, to determine if you would or would not like to proceed.

Suggestions for first dates:

Brunch on the weekend: This daytime activity provides a good opportunity to get to know each other in a casual setting. The food, the presence of other people, and a lively atmosphere gives you the chance to observe someone without the pressure of constant one-on-one conversation.

Physical activities: Jogging, horseback, or bicycle riding, sailing, walking, etc., are healthy for you. Some people find it relaxing when engaging in physical activities; in such settings, conversations flow naturally and spontaneously. Whether a future friendship develops or not, people will usually remember activities which they shared with someone.

Coffee or lunch date: These are excellent time savers for first meetings. Sometimes you can tell from the beginning that a person will not be suitable for you. In such a case, you can terminate the meeting quickly by ordering something simple like a coffee or cold sandwich. A simple lunch or coffee date is also relatively inexpensive; neither one will feel obligated or pressured regardless of the way things turn out.

First date tips

Like every important event in your life, it helps to be prepared before you go out on a date. It is natural to feel uncomfortable, anxious, and a little insecure because you want to make the best possible impression on your date.

If you are a woman, you must keep in mind you are not out to convince a man to fall in love with you. Instead, you are interviewing a man to see if he qualifies for the position of being your long-term companion. Think of yourself as a high-powered software programmer who has already turned down numerous lucrative job offers. At a job interview, you are not there to see if the company is going to offer you a position; you are there to see if the working conditions at this company suit you. This is exactly the position you are in when dating and you should act this way at all times.

Here are some suggestions to make you relaxed so you can truly enjoy the occasion.

For women:

Dress comfortably. It is best to wear something you already own and which makes you feel attractive and comfortable. Choose something people have complemented you on. Don't rush out and buy a new outfit, then spend the entire evening wondering if you look good in it.

A woman I know said she was so overcome with nervousness on a date that she blurted out, "Look, I don't know if I can stand this any longer, I'm so nervous." Her sympathetic date finally said, "You know what? I am nervous too." They both laughed and the rest of the evening went smoothly.

Use your own transportation. Take no chances, especially when you are meeting a complete stranger. If you don't drive, take a cab or use public transport. When you meet your date in neutral territory, he has no way of knowing where you live. This proves helpful in the unfortunate event that things do not work out and your date decides to pursue you regardless. Also, if things are not what you expected, you could bail out early and not feel trapped. Even if everything goes well, you will be spared the inconveniences of the ever-lingering questions, "Should I or should I not invite him in?" or "Would he respect me in the morning?"

Be moderate with your expectations. Remember that you are on a date to meet someone new and share his company while enjoying an activity. Don't go with the expectation that this will be **the one**, because you will be disappointed if he is not. If you go into a date with extremely high expectations, you are sure to feel less than happy with the actual results.

Have something to talk about. Read a current newspaper or magazine so you can be up-to-date with current events. Start a conversation like: "Do you think American relations with the Middle East will significantly affect the American investment climate?" Women who are knowledgeable about topical events impress most men. His response to your conversation may also give you an idea of his areas of interest.

Don't be nervous when there's silence. Stay calm, make eye contact, exhibit confidence. You don't have to fill every moment with conversation. Some people are uncomfortable with silence and immediately begin to blurt out information to fill the gap. It's not necessary.

For men:

Call before you leave to pick up your date. Your date will appreciate this. Most women like to make a stunning impression especially on a first meeting. They prefer to "emerge" when they are ready instead of being rushed or forced to sit around waiting for their date to show up.

Make plans before hand. The words "Uh...what would you like to do?" is interpreted by most women as laziness, poor organizational skills, or lack of excitement or concern about the event. Knowing how you would like to entertain your date is a sign of confidence and responsibility. Be assertive.

It is sometimes better to suggest two or three alternatives in case your date may have special preferences. "Would you like to eat Italian, French, or Japanese food?" When you ask ahead of time, your date would be able to dress appropriately. Imagine wearing a cocktail dress when you made plans to go rollerblading.

Don't go overboard. Some guys rent a limousine, purchase costly gifts, or take their dates to the most expensive restaurant in town. Depending on who you are, this might be a fun gesture, but most women serious about finding lasting love, consider such actions unnecessary and sometimes even in bad taste.

Out on a date

While you always plan to enjoy yourself, remember that the primary purpose for first dates is to gather information. As quickly as possible, learn as much as you can about your newfound acquaintance. The more you know about a person, the quicker you will be able to make a reasonable evaluation as to whether he/she can meet your requirements. Of course you cannot obtain all the information you need on the first meeting, and I am not suggesting that you turn your date into an inquisition. But simple questioning that shows genuine interest will put you on the right track.

In your search for lasting love, time is your most valuable resource; use it wisely. Try not to spend a lot of time on conventional dating activities such as parties, movies, and concerts. Your time would be better spent in places where the ambience lends itself to intimate conversations. Carol, a fashion model who lives in Los Angeles, said it took her years of dating before she realized why she was not in a stable relationship even though she wanted to be. She said. "It seemed that men believed they had to impress me. Every time there was a special event, live concert, grand opening, television award show in town, I would receive various invitations to accompany men. For a while, I was flattered by all the attention and expensive gifts. It took me some time to realize that I was not getting to know anyone on an intimate basis. I don't mean sexual intimacy; there were plenty of offers for that."

"Perhaps it was because most of my dates were busy people, but I never got close enough to any man to really know him. Imagine the position of a woman attempting to initiate action intended to bring her closer to having a steady relationship with a man. Most men would run in the other direction. I was on a date one evening when it hit me. Most of my dates were men who, for whatever reason, pursued me. I then decided to initiate getting to know those I thought were attractive and might be suitable for me. It took me about six months before I began dating Joe with whom I have had a wonderful relationship for the past year."

Lead the conversation

Women, some guys may be reluctant to open up to you immediately. Perhaps they are self conscious about bombarding you with information about themselves, would like to be courteous and let you speak, or are just plain shy. If he seems hesitant to open up, take the initiative. Say, "I accepted a job in this city five months ago. My company gave me a choice of a six-month trial or returning to my old job. I've made several new friends here and I think the city is wonderful. I've decided to stay. How about you? Have you been living here long?"

Guide him in a direction where he would reveal himself to you. With practice, you will learn to ask the right questions so he is not even aware you are interviewing him. Within a couple of hours, you should be able to decide if he is suitable enough for a second date.

Not what you expected?

Your first impression of a person is usually a good indicator of his/her true personality. Sometimes you can tell within a few minutes of meeting that someone is unsuitable for you. Should this be the case, it is better not to reveal your true feelings at that moment. You wouldn't want to hurt someone's feelings. Pass the time as best as you can in the given circumstances. Of course you should try to bring the date to an end as soon an opportunity presents itself by saying, "I've got a tough day ahead of me tomorrow; I want to have an early night." While you don't want to be rude, your time is better spent preparing for your next encounter.

Ending it smoothly

There comes a time (whether it's after a first date or even after you have been seeing someone for a while) you decide finally, no, definitely not interested. How do you end it without hurting the other person's feelings?

Remember that brutal honesty is not necessary here, so statements like, "I was misled by your voice on the telephone. I had a different conception of your looks," or "I would prefer to stay home and defrost my refrigerator than listen to one more of your mortician jokes" should never cross your lips.

Instead, give the impression that a new situation has developed and it makes it difficult for you to continue the relationship. "My ex-girlfriend is asking me to give our relationship another chance" or "Since this new manager took over, I am being forced to put in some exceptionally long hours." Make it seem like you are thinking about it just at this moment and that you did not plan the date just to give him/her the bad news. "I guess that's why I've not been good company lately. This has been on my mind for some time now."

Once the point is firmly stated, you don't have to offer further explanations. The other person will know it's a breakup and will appreciate your consideration handling it this way. You can go on to say, "I was having so much fun with you; it's a pity things turned out like this. I will miss you."

Note. This strategy should not be used on someone with whom you had a serious relationship for some time. Breaking up with a mate with whom you were romantically connected should be treated with great sincerity and tenderness, and would require a lot of time.

When you are the rejected one

If, for whatever reason, you find yourself in the position of being rejected, consider these points.

First of all, believe and accept the breakup. Understand that even though you are not what he/she wanted for a love companion, he/she still likes and respects you as a human being. Do not think for a moment, "He was so nice about it, maybe he just needs some more time." No, he does not need more time. He definitely does not want to be involved with you. Deal with it.

There may be an opening for you to be friends if you so desire. Remember, he may truly like you. Don't ruin it. If, for instance, he calls you sometime afterwards, do not take this as a sign he has changed his mind and wants to continue dating you. More than likely, this is not the case.

I've known women who simply change their telephone number to break off with a guy, so consider it a compliment when a woman takes the time and effort to let you down nicely. Whether you like it or not, face the reality that you cannot fit everyone's taste.

Managing your activities

Once you meet someone with relationship potential, your next step is to spend more time getting to know him/her better. This section is directed mostly to women because most men don't find it necessary to manage romantic activities aggressively. Men should, however, be aware that romance is no different than, for example, a construction project. It requires planning, implementation and periodic review, until completion.

Your objective:

For any undertaking to be successful, start by defining clear goals and objectives. You've heard the saying, "If you don't know where you're going, how will you get there?" Similarly, you must know what kind of relationship you want. Do you want a companion to satisfy your romantic needs while you complete your studies toward a career? Are you looking for a long-term relationship? If so, what kind? Perhaps a live-in companion at your side while you climb the corporate ladder? Or someone to take care of your romantic and financial security? Or marriage and a family life?

Having clear objectives accomplishes the following:

You can eliminate people who are clearly not suitable for you from your list of prospects. Women tend to date haphazardly, especially when they are constantly being approached for dates. The result is that some women spend a lot of time on guys who are simply not right for them but "so what, I'm having a good time anyway," they say.

Even if it takes time to find the exact partner you are seeking, knowing your objectives keeps you on track. Whenever you come into contact with someone, you will always be acting in your best interest, i.e., keeping focused on what you want.

Setting a time limit

In addition to knowing what they want, some women set a time limit on their objectives. Sometimes this works well because it forces them to rigidly manage limited resources and quickly eliminate unsuitable situations.

Debbie, a dental technician in Toronto, had been dating Frank, a salesman, for about a year and a half. She said that setting a time limit helped her to escape a dead-end relationship.

"I decided to go steady with Frank because I felt he was the kind of man I would like to marry. We did many things together and he always talked about settling down some day to have a family. It's not that I didn't believe him, nor was I in a hurry to get married; I was only 25 and knew there was plenty of time. After reading a book on marriage, I decided to set a time limit of eight months for a marriage commitment. I didn't tell Frank about my decision because I didn't want him to feel pressured.

I would periodically bring up the subject and, like always, he would say he is not ready yet. When the eight months arrived, I stuck to my decision and stopped seeing Frank. Not long afterward I started dating other guys. Now I am seeing men who seem much more serious than Frank about sharing their lives with me."

"Frank has tried to get back with me many times, but I feel that I've moved on and have no desire to go back with him. I am much happier now, especially since I have a wider selection of guys to choose from."

Keeping records

When you actively date several guys, you may find it difficult to keep track of the information you gather on each individual. Here is where your dating diary comes in handy. Start by creating a personality profile on each person you date and keep updating it as you gather more information.

Keeping records sometimes helps your date feel comfortable opening up to you because he sees you are genuinely interested in what he has to say. Consider this scenario: Your date once mentioned briefly he still maintains contact with a childhood acquaintance named David. This was much earlier in your dating relationship but you made a note in your diary. Now you want to find out more about his early childhood, but you are not sure how to approach the subject. So you begin something like this: "How old were you when your friend David came to live in your neighborhood?" Your date will be impressed at your ability to recall details and may begin speaking freely about his childhood.

Setting limits and boundaries

When it is clear in your mind what you want in a relationship, you will be able to identify the kind of mate that is right for you.

Your next step is to sketch a general profile of your ideal mate and clearly list the areas in which you will not compromise. This list should be written down and in your possession at all times to avoid getting sidetracked. Many women say they know what kind of mate they need, but in a moment of impulse, they select men who are clearly inappropriate for them. Of course, they regret this later but only after time and emotional energy have been wasted.

In a subtle but firm manner, let a mate know as soon as possible the extent of your limits, i.e., what you will and will not accept under any circumstances. He/she must know, for example, that your time is valuable and would need advance notice before any social arrangements can be made.

Here's an example for women. A man may call at 7 p.m. on Friday and say, "Listen I just had an idea. Why don't we go nightclubbing this evening? I can pick you up in one and a half hours. What do you say?" To you, the spontaneity may seem exciting, so you accept. Yet, even if you are dying to go out with someone, it is best to decline his invitation. Accepting an invitation under such circumstances sets a pattern, which may lead to disrespect. The man may believe either you find him extremely irresistible or that your opportunities for dating are limited and you are happy to go out with anyone who comes along.

Juanita, 33, lives in Miami. She says she can always gauge the level of interest a man has in her by the way he makes dating plans. "If he tries to make arrangements to go out with me on a Friday or Saturday night, I believe he considers me an important date. If, on the other hand, he continually tries to fit me in his Monday to Thursday schedule, I assume I am not his first choice."

Many women are at a loss for an explanation when men lose interest in them. This would not be so difficult to understand if you knew people respect you when you know what you want and are not afraid to ask. If you let a man know how to treat you, he will do his best to live up to your expectations. If you make no demands of him, especially at the beginning of the relationship, he assumes that anything goes and soon falls into bad habits.

From the results of our survey, it seems that in addition to physical beauty men also need mental stimulation to maintain their interest in women. In the initial stages of dating, a man subconsciously seeks this stimulation. If you as a woman make it easy for him to gain access to you, you rob him of the challenge. In the absence of challenge, a man gets bored, loses interest, and moves on.

Establishing boundaries and enforcing them shows a man you have a high regard for yourself. Women who clearly possess high self-esteem receive more favorable treatment from men. You would be considered one of his preferred choices for a serious relationship, not just a casual date. Some casual dates remain this way forever.

CHAPTER FIVE
Getting to know your partner better

Females seeking a male love partner are addressed in this chapter, but this applies equally to men. Too often, men become overwhelmed by attractive women. In the initial stages of the relationship, men spend so much time in pursuit of a woman that they seem to overlook basic factors in a woman's behavior. It appears that men believe that, because a woman is attractive, everything will fall into place. But women, don't be misled by this. Whether they choose to admit it or not, men and women alike have a list of needs and desires.

In their conscious and subconscious minds, men know what they are looking for in a mate. These preferences have been developed over a lifetime due to upbringing, influences, and experiences. If a man grew up in a home in which family life was important, his ideal woman may be one that fulfills the role of a good mother to his children. Perhaps his mother was a career woman. In such case, he may be fascinated by a female who is organized and pays attention to details. So without changing your personality, try to understand his needs and let him know you can fulfill them, if you believe you can and want to do so. Remember, even though it may seem that way, being attractive is not enough to sustain a serious relationship.

Say you have narrowed your prospects down to one, maybe two or three individuals. These are "candidates" you find acceptable. On the surface, they possess some of the basic qualities you seek in a mate, e.g., physical appearance, good social standing, good conversationalist, etc. You feel sufficiently attracted to one or all of these candidates that you can easily fall in love. Now you are anxious to find out (a.) Do you share enough compatibility to sustain a long lasting relationship? (b.) Does your new-found companion feel the same way and is ready to fall in love with you?

How do you get to this point? You learn as much as you can about him/her through constant interviewing. The interviewing process should be as casual as possible and part of your regular conversations. Ask questions that encourage your mate to reveal himself/herself to you. You cannot love someone you don't know.

Learning as much as you can about a prospective love partner helps you decide whether you can comfortably live with him/her. To many, it would seem like common sense to learn as much as we can about a person before we enter into a relationship. So, why is it that so many people neglect to ask questions about a person with whom they may decide to spend a great part of their lives?

We are afraid of the answers we might receive. Women, when you meet a handsome, eligible guy, the last thing you want to hear is that he has some kind of fault. To you he seems perfect; in your mind, you would like him to stay that way. You may also tell yourself; "No matter what's wrong with him, I can change that fault if he falls in love with me."

Shelley won several beauty contests in her home town before she was 27. Soon after she came to live in New York, she began dating Giovanni, a 34-year-old businessman who immediately swept Shelley off her feet. Many of her friends told her Giovanni is a womanizer and not likely to settle down with any one woman.

It's not that she didn't believe her friends, but Shelley has always shown a high level of self-confidence. She believed Giovanni would fall for her and possibly ask her to be his wife. She never discussed the idea of marriage with Giovanni because she thought he would bring up the subject when he was ready. After several months of dating and Giovanni did not propose to her, she became anxious but was now afraid to discuss the future of their relationship with him. She was beginning to realize that, even though she had enjoyed his friendship, her time could have been better spent with someone like herself who wanted to settle down.

When it became clear Giovanni had no intentions of proposing to her, she decided to bring up the subject. He explained he was far from ready for marriage and thought she also wanted to enjoy life now and settle down later.

"I realize now that I was truly afraid to learn that Giovanni in fact may not have been suitable for me. But since I was having such a good time, why spoil it, I thought. Now, I see that the time lost could have been better spent in the pursuit of what I really want."

You do not want to answer questions about yourself. People who are unsure of themselves are afraid to reveal something about their past or are uncomfortable with some aspects of their character. They may avoid entering into detailed discussion with a prospective mate. It's like an unspoken agreement: "I won't investigate you if you don't ask me too many questions about my life." This might be okay when you first meet someone, but leaving out important details about yourself when considering a serious relationship is a recipe for future problems.

Susan, 25, was abandoned by her parents when she was two years old. She spent most of her early childhood in an orphanage. In spite of her misfortune, she had always been a bright student. Recently, she obtained her college diploma.

Susan avoids discussions about her parents. Whenever the subject came up, she would say that both her parents had died in a car accident. She has always wanted to get married and settle down, but most of her relationships ended prematurely. Susan believed she was not equal to other people because her parents did not want her as a child. This belief has been a source of unhappiness and sometimes depression for most of her adult life. Most of the men in her life were stable and eligible; they too wanted a permanent relationship. She could not understand why relationships did not work for her.

So she started dating Michael, a 32-year-old salesman, one summer. After about eight months, they decided to live together and had plans to get married in the future. Susan liked Michael and desperately hoped that, this time, things would work out for them. Whenever she goes in one of her depression moods, however, she would keep to herself for days. This had always been a source of quarrels with her previous lovers who had eventually grown tired of the situation and left.

Michael was patient with her; though, consoling her during her depression while trying without success to understand the source of the problem. This went on for several months until Michael insisted she needed some professional help. Of course, she refused and claimed that this was her nature and said she would be fine when the depression passes. Against her wishes and unknown to her, Michael contacted a psychotherapist and made several appointments, which had to be cancelled because Susan refused to go.

One evening, Michael came home from work and

announced he was leaving the relationship unless Susan immediately agreed to see the psychotherapist. She became hysterical and begged Michael not to leave her. Eventually, he got her to agree to keep an appointment with the therapist. Michael attended all the sessions with her until the therapist requested Susan attend the sessions alone.

After several sessions, the therapist called Michael at work and asked him to come over to her office. He entered the office and saw Susan sitting on the couch. The therapist asked him to sit beside Susan because she had something to say to him. With tears in her eyes, Susan began to tell Michael all about her childhood and how she grew up in an orphanage. She asked his forgiveness for not opening up to him before.

Michael was calm about the whole thing and told her everything would be all right. Shortly afterward, Susan stopped seeing the therapist and no longer had spells of depression.

Susan and Michael are much happier together now and have already set the date for their wedding. She thanked him for being so patient with her and for saving their relationship. Michael confessed that he had no intentions of leaving, but only told her so to force her to get help.

Don't be afraid to be up front

Of course, a person may have several traits and habits you are not comfortable with. But being aware of these beforehand gives you the opportunity to compromise before you make a serious commitment. Putting it simply, if you let your mate know some of his actions make you uncomfortable, he may make an effort to modify those actions. Failing to bring up these facts in the early stages of the courtship could result in confusion and possible resentment later.

Consider this scenario: In the early stages of your relationship, you always tried to make your boyfriend feel comfortable when he visited you. He liked to watch the ball game during dinner, so you served him meals in front of the television. You sat with him and seemed to enjoy the event equally.

Now that you are married, you announce that dinner must be eaten at the table and you believe he spends too much time watching games. Imagine his surprise about this new development. He asks himself, "What happened to that sweet woman, my buddy who liked to sit and watch the game with me?" He may believe you were being nice to him only because you wanted him to marry you. He may even grow to resent you for this behavior.

Getting him to open up to you

If a man feels you are conducting an interview with him, he may be reluctant to speak candidly. A barrage of direct questions may cause him to clam up. A good way to make him feel comfortable is to show him you want to learn more about him because he seems interesting. You can say, "You know, when I heard of your achievements at such an early age, I was so fascinated that I could not wait to meet you. Tell me, what made you decide to become a military man?"

There will be hundreds of questions you need to ask, but do this over a period of time and always appear to be spontaneous. If, for instance, you are out for a drive in the countryside, you can comment on the surrounding beauty, saying, "I enjoy being in the countryside; I guess it's because I grew up on a farm. Tell me about your childhood. Where did you grow up?"

To get to know a man better, ask him about his past and his plans for the future. People are always ready to tell the stories about their past, especially if they are happy with their achievements so far. He'll be happy, for example, to talk about when he got a whopping promotion in his job or how he assisted in designing a new inventory system for the factory where he worked.

As he unfolds his life story, listen carefully. You will be able to understand many aspects of his character: where he sees himself today, where he plans to be in the future, and what other people think about him. If you show genuine interest in what he is saying, he is more likely to open up to you. You will be able to learn what is important to him. The more he tells you, the closer he will be drawn to you, making it easy for him to confide in you about future plans.

Don't be timid to bring up controversial subjects such as religion, sex, and politics. His views and attitudes toward these subjects will tell you whether you would want to have a relationship with him or not. If, for example, you discover that he is a devout Muslim, you may want to know if some of his religious customs would conflict with your lifestyle and beliefs.

A word about listening

Listening is not a passive process. No one expects you to sit in a subservient manner listening without interacting. Yes, you will be silent when you need to be, but you should show interest by participating. When he completes a story, make comments such as, "I like that; tell me more." Or "That must have been a very exciting part of your life." Show him you are not bored (except of course if you are, in which case you should move on). It would be difficult to have a blissful relationship with someone who bores you from the beginning.

How do you know if you can believe what he says?

Even though most people are honest, you have to be on your guard against being misled by what a man says. Most people are guilty of a little exaggeration, especially when talking about achievements. Then, some people deliberately deceive you to gain your friendship. So in addition to paying attention to everything he says, also listen to what he does not say. For instance, if he tells you he lives with his mother and after four months of dating, he avoids taking you to his home, he may not be telling you the whole story.

Action speaks louder than words

To please you, a man may tell you how much he adores children, that he would have no problem sharing his life with your children. On observation, however, you notice that his countenance changes whenever your kids are present. He smiles and tries to be nice, but you can see he is extremely uncomfortable in their presence. It may be that he is initially nervous and needs more time to interact with the kids. It could also mean he has negative feelings about being a father to someone else's children.

So if your relationship with such a man includes your children, consider the situation closely. You can do this by creating situations where he must interact with the kids, then observe his reactions over a period of time. Sooner or later, you will discover his true feelings.

Evasive actions

A man may change the topic, get defensive, or avoid certain kinds of discussions altogether. If the topic of discussion is of great importance to you, try to determine the reasons he's evading the subject. Neglecting to do so can be the cause of future problems.

Shannon, an office assistant, decided to seek counseling after three years of marriage. She said. "I should have known that something was not right with Jack. From the time we started dating, something was missing. Jack was nice and treated me well. He is a responsible person and we had a lot of laughs together. But sometimes he would sit by himself very quietly. When I asked him if something was bothering him, he would always say he has a couple of matters at work he has to take care of, but nothing he can't handle.

"At first, this seemed okay, but then I realized that, apart from a few details about his work, he never tells me how he feels about anything. I remembered we had a discussion about saying the words "I love you." He believes people don't have to go around saying "I love you." If you love someone, you show it, not say it. The more I thought about it, the more I realized Jack has never told me his true feelings.

"The thought of this was driving me crazy, so I tried several times to speak to Jack about it. He explained that he knows what he feels and does not see the need to continually talk about his feelings. He also says he does not like to burden others with his personal problems. This matter became the reason for many quarrels between us, and we would not speak to each other for days at a time. Our sex lives became non-existent and I began thinking of leaving him. Some of my friends told me I should be happy that I have such a kind, responsible man like Jack, but I knew I could not continue living with a man who was emotionally shut down.

"When I suggested that we go for counseling, he became furious and said, 'Now you feel that we should expose our personal problems to a complete stranger? Not me.' Fortunately, my counselor was experienced and showed me a way to get Jack to accompany me to counseling sessions. We discovered that Jack's lack of emotional openness was due to certain childhood experiences. After several months of counseling, Jack has already begun to show a great deal of improvement. He and I talk about everything now and have a much better sex life than before."

Don't make a premature decision

If you think your man is leaving out important information about himself, or you discover things about him that bother you, make notes for later reference. Do not attempt to enter discussions about these matters immediately, nor make a premature decision to rule him out as ineligible. Instead, continue to seek more information over a period of time. Make sure you have not misjudged the situation or overreacted.

When you feel you have gathered all the information in your own way, decide whether or not you can be a couple. Remember, you cannot be 100% compatible with anyone, but if a man scores about 75% on your eligibility scale, you have a good chance of making it together.

Chapter Six
Things to know before you fall in love

Here are some topics to include in your discussion with your prospective mate.

Career

A man's career is of great importance when considering a serious relationship. What the man does has a strong impact not only on himself, but also on his mate. Consider this.

You run into an old friend you haven't seen for a while. She tells you she is engaged to be married. One of the first questions that comes to mind is, "What does your fiancé do for a living?" Your friend says, "He is an industrial engineer with a large chemical company." You say, "Congratulations, you've done well." On the other hand, I am sure you have heard other replies to this question, such as. "He is a traffic cop but he is taking night courses to become a lawyer." Or "He is only a salesman now but they promised to make him sales manager within the year."

Even today, society values people according to their career achievements, a man is considered a "good catch" if he has a prestigious career. This value system, however, may have some foundation. A recent study of about 2000 marriages in the United States showed that women who married well-educated men were more successful than others who didn't. Researchers found that the wives of men of higher status enjoyed happier marriages, had more children, and were less likely to get divorced than the wives of lower status men. [17]

You should, therefore, determine if a prospective mate is where he wants to be in his career. Also, you, as his companion are comfortable with what he does for a living and his status in the community. Some women say they are attracted to men who hold high positions in their jobs.

In a counseling session, Stephanie, 35, confessed that her appetite for sex with her husband decreased considerably when she learned he had failed (for the second time) the final exam for his Securities and Exchange Commission license. At the time of their marriage, Jack worked as a clerk in a brokerage office, but his goal was to become a stockbroker. She believes now he just doesn't have what it takes to be a stockbroker. "I haven't said anything to Jack, but I just don't feel turned on as before during sex. Jack doesn't seem as exciting to me as he used to."

Conversely, although a man may want to marry you, he may hesitate because he might feel he has not yet reached where he would like to be in his career. He may decide he should go back to school for a couple of years. You will have to decide, if you are prepared to postpone your wedding plans for this length of time, and if he would still want to marry you after he graduates.

You should also be aware of his long-range goals. If his ultimate intention is to pursue research projects in the Rain Forest of South America, you may be confronted with being separated for considerable lengths of time or abandoning your own goals altogether to be with him.

Your chances for success in a relationship increase when you love your mate for the way he is now and not for the way you believe he may be tomorrow.
—Peter Hector

Questions to consider.

- Is he a workaholic?
- Does he have the potential to achieve his goals, or is he a dreamer?
- Would his chosen career produce enough financial resources to sustain the quality of life you want? (This would be an important consideration if you ever decide to work part-time or quit work altogether to start a family.)
- Does he respect your career?

Education

If you grew up in a household in which parents placed great emphasis on academic achievements, you may understand why some people attribute a high value to formal education. School teachers, college professors, and similar professionals would consider it a great disappointment if a member of their household is unable to achieve academic qualifications. It's wise to find out if the man you are dating is a product of such environment.

Try to understand early in a relationship your prospective mate's view on academic achievements. If he is much more educated than you, he may like you as a date but may not consider you eligible for a long-term love partner.

Determine how rigid his views are on this subject. It is easy to understand why a wide gap in education levels would produce a lack of mental stimulation and ultimate boredom, but intelligent people know that college degrees do not tell the whole story.

There may be logical reasons why someone did not complete his/her academic agendas. Loss of a family member, financial disaster, or serious illness can sometimes be the cause. If, for instance, you discover that a man is less educated than you, do not write him off as ineligible. Instead, talk to him, listen to the way he arranges his thoughts, how he communicates with you, and how he analyzes things. He might surprise you. I'm sure you have heard of heads of successful companies who do not possess a university degree, yet their knowledge and intelligence extend to areas far beyond their normal realm of business.

If, however, you decide to select a man less educated than you, do not expect that you will improve his education level. This situation is common with women who believe a man can change his ideals if he finds a woman he truly loves. This is usually not true. You may rationalize, "He's okay but I would be happier if he completes his business degree." Remember, no matter what he says, he will complete his business degree only if he wants to. If you pressure him, he will resent you later. So, if you truly believe you cannot possibly live with someone less educated than you, find someone closer to your ideals.

Money matters

Whatever your outlook on money, you will need to determine your partner's general attitude toward finances and compare them. Depending on his upbringing, a man may have set ideas about money. Perhaps he has been taught that money should be spent only to acquire the necessities of life and the balance put away for a rainy day. Perhaps he believes in long-term planning, e.g., saving up until he has the money to buy a new television instead of using his credit card to acquire it immediately.

Such a person may resent a woman who is a lot freer than he is in her spending habits. It could also be that the woman spends conservatively while the man is the extravagant one. It is best to know each other's spending habits beforehand because of the importance money plays in everyday living. And remember that once you enter into a love relationship, money management becomes a joint affair. A University of Denver study on "What couples fight about in America" puts money as the number one cause, followed by a tie between communications and sex. Some people put sex in the number-two position and communications in number three, while others reverse the order. [18]

You may think that money will be a problem only among couples struggling to make ends meet. Surprisingly, when researchers took into account people in higher income groups and wealthy people, they concluded that money is a problem, regardless of the size of income levels. The question of financial matters is a day-to-day issue and touches every aspect of our lives. On top of that are major financial issues like buying a home and saving for retirement. Such matters can alter the quality of one's life on a long-term basis.

Money plays an important part in many other issues in a relationship. Many of these issues are hidden and do not surface as money issues which can sometimes be confusing to the parties concerned. For example, in the question of power struggles, the partner with the most money can use this position to gain the edge.

Things to consider:

- When a man is frugal in his spending habits, it can affect you in various ways. You may, for example, like to wear designer clothing, which he may consider a waste of money. Or you may want to send your kids to private schools but he may believe the additional expense is not justifiable. Such matters can be a constant source of disagreement, even if you earn enough and are willing to pay for the things you like.

- Some guys are extravagant and like to shower you with expensive gifts, luxurious vacations, etc. That's fine if he can truly afford it. You will, however, have to consider whether you would have to bear some of the cost of such expensive habits once you enter into a love partnership.

Family background

Samuel Jack is 87 years old. I asked him what would be the most important advice he can give to someone thinking about getting married. He said, "Get to know his or her family. Find out as much as you can by speaking to the mother, father, brothers, and sisters. Also ask other people's opinion of that person—where and how someone grows up has a lot to do with who they are today."

The messages about relationships that a child receives while growing up usually influence the way that child handles his/her own relationships. For instance, some men are extremely uncomfortable showing physical affection to their mates in the presence of other people. Upon investigation, you may find that, while he was growing up, he never saw his father show affection to his mother because his father believed that exposing inner feelings is a sign of weakness.

Usually men who have had a close relationship with their mothers while growing up are more kind and loving. They are more likely to have a high regard for women than men who didn't.

In my travels through Latin America and my associations with people from that region, I've observed that men of Latin American origin share an exceptional closeness to their mothers. Local sources informed me that in Latin cultures, a mother generally assumes total financial and emotional responsibility in the upbringing of her children. In some South American societies, men leave home for long periods in search of work opportunities. A man could be gone for a year or more, and in some cases abandon his family altogether.

In Venezuela where I lived for seven years, there is a popular saying: "Madre es una sola, Padre es cualquiera." Translated, this is a reminder to children that, no matter what, their mothers will always be there for them, unlike fathers who may not always be present. Imagine the state of mind of a child who, from a very young age, sees his mother constantly struggle to provide life's basic necessities. The child may see his father infrequently, so he is forced to depend on his mother for love, care, and emotional support. Such a child grows up with enormous admiration, respect, and love not only for his mother, but also for all women.

Sometimes, however, the bond, that exists between a mother and son can have negative effects on a love relationship. Mothers usually place a high value on their sons and, in many cases, attempt to influence their son's decision in the selection of a wife. Women who have had to deal with their partner's mother at some time have experienced the feeling that mothers believe if you are anything less than Princess Diana, you are not good enough for their son.

This common phenomenon with moms is generally accepted by most women. What is difficult to accept, though, is a man who has not gained independence from his mother. Some men continue to look to their mothers for guidance even after they have grown up and left home. This can be a sign of serious psychological problems and may require help from a trained professional.

So, if he always brings up his mother in every conversation and you discover he has to call her at least three times a day because she is lonely, watch out. He might be a mama's boy, which can have adverse effects on your relationship.

Availability

To clarify the meaning of availability when it comes to relationships, here is the definition: Someone who is not presently married, living with, or romantically involved with another person and in all other ways free to enter into a love relationship can be considered available.

When a potential partner tells you that "I am seeing someone, but we are in the process of separating," or "I am living with someone, for convenience, but we no longer have sex," or that "I don't love her anymore, but every time I try to leave she says she'll kill herself," he is probably not ready to consider another relationship. To many, it seems like common sense that people seeking a committed relationship should stay away from someone who is clearly not available to commit. So why is it that so many people find themselves with love mates who are, in fact, not free to commit to anyone?

Reasons vary from case to case, but psychological research indicates these three possibilities: [19]

1. Reliving childhood experiences

A person who felt abandoned by parents as a child attempts to repeat childhood experiences by selecting mates who cannot be available, Psychologists say such a person never succeeded in getting needed attention as a child; hence the subconscious mind continues this pattern of seeking attention as an adult. The complication here is that the adult is reliving childhood experiences and does not necessarily need attention. If the unavailable partner suddenly becomes available, usually he/she loses appeal as a prospective mate. The seeker then finds another mate who is also unavailable and begins the process all over again.

2. Afraid of commitment

Even though some people may consciously seek a relationship, their subconscious minds guide them toward partners who are not in a position to offer a commitment to them. Why? Because, subconsciously they are afraid of intimacy, so being in a relationship with an unavailable mate protects them from the intimacy they fear so much.

A child who was in some way abused by a trusted and respected adult may have suffered emotional damage. Usually such violation leaves deep emotional scars, which remain with the child into adulthood.

As an adult, that child may go to great lengths to avoid intimacy, believing that closeness to anyone could only produce pain and emotional suffering. On the surface, such a person genuinely believes he/she wants an intimate relationship but the subconscious being works in the background, sabotaging genuine efforts to find an intimate partner.

3. Low self-Esteem

At some point in their lives, perhaps in childhood or young adulthood, some people might have had experiences that caused them to believe they are not as worthy as other humans. Such adults may accept an unavailable partner because they believe they do not deserve a mate all for themselves.

Children who were products of dysfunctional homes may grow up to be adults who suffer from varying levels of self-esteem deficiency. Even well-intentioned parents sometimes lack the knowledge needed to raise their children to be well-adjusted adults. [20]

No doubt you have heard parents saying to their children, "You will never amount to anything in life." or "You're going to become a bum just like your brother." Although intended to shock a child into improving unacceptable behavior, psychoanalysts say such comments sometimes have negative effects on the minds of children. A child may grow up believing he/she is not good enough to be equal to other people. As an adult, he/she will be content to accept whatever he/she can get when seeking a love partner.

Other unavailable prospects

If you are considering a relationship with a person who is separated or divorced, be aware of the following:

Separated

A person separated from his/her mate can decide to return to the relationship at any time. Depending on the length of time of the separation, you will have to determine how strong this possibility is. Sometimes a partner needs time and breathing space to consider if a relationship is worth saving.

During this period of review, a person may be in a vulnerable state of mind and send confusing signals. For example, you may believe someone has a strong attraction to you when, in fact, he/she only needs a shoulder to cry on. In any case, a separated person will have many issues to deal with and is rarely in a state of mind to consider a new relationship.

Divorced

For most people, a divorce is a traumatic event. It can be extremely difficult to determine the mental state of a divorced person. A divorcee may still be in mourning for the "ex" and is not yet free to consider a new relationship. In many cases, a person on the rebound (i.e., coming out of one relationship and entering into another) may be attracted to you because you possess qualities that are different to his/her previous mate.

For instance, if a woman's previous partner was a workaholic and had little time for enjoyment, she may gravitate to a mate who is more easy-going than her husband and knows how to enjoy life. Because the new partner satisfies an immediate need, she may believe "this is the one." She could discover later that, since her last relationship, she might have undergone many mental changes. Things she once considered important, were no longer a priority in her life.

Joe, an industrial chemist, constantly fought with his "ex" because she was too extravagant in her spending habits. After the break up, he became attracted to and started dating Anna who was frugal with money. Things went well and they started living together. After several months, Joe received a large insurance settlement, the kind of money that could set him up for life. Within four months of receiving his good fortune, he broke off the relationship with Anna. Joe discovered that he became less and less attracted to her. He then realized that his initial attraction was based on the fact that she was a good money manager, which was important for him at the time. Now that he no longer had a money problem, he was clearly able to see he had chosen Anna for the wrong reasons.

If children are involved in the marriage, it may take a much longer time to sever emotional ties with your "ex." Custody arrangements, visiting privileges and continuing concerns for the children's welfare usually keep an individual connected to an ex-spouse even after a divorce has been finalized.

A man may have to provide financial support for the children, depending on their ages and the economic situation of his wife. Remember, with marriage the woman automatically takes on his financial responsibilities. If she wanted to have kids of her own, would he be financially capable of assisting in the support of a new family while supporting his children? What if she has children of her own? How do both of them feel about bringing up the two families together?

People who have gone through a divorce may be even better candidates for new relationships because they have learned a great deal from their previous ones, one hopes! It's somewhat easier to find what works for you when you already know what doesn't work.

You probably know people who find lasting love after one or more attempts. There is no reason you cannot be one of them. Statistics show that most men remarry within three to four years of a divorce. [21] It is extremely important, however, to confirm that a divorced person is truly available, and committed before any serious involvement can be considered.

Similarities in values and goals

When it comes to seeking a relationship, do opposites really attract? Can people who possess different sets of goals and values find compatibility with each other? Dr Neil Clark Warren, clinical psychologist and author of *How to know if someone is worth pursuing in two dates or less* suggests being cautious if the qualities that attract you to someone are different from your own. He explains that, while opposites often attract initially, they usually drive each other crazy over the long haul.

Say you meet someone with whom you are considering having a long-term loving relationship. You find that, like yourself, your potential partner is clear about his/her values, goals, and lifestyle choices. What happens if these choices are different from yours? Let's say that you adore children and can hardly wait to settle down and have a family. Your partner, on the other hand, likes children but prefers to pursue a career first and start a family later. What if your partner is adventurous, likes to travel, and is fascinated by new cultures and meeting new people. But you find comfort living in a small city where you can enjoy a much quieter life.

Dr Nathaniel Branden, a foremost authority in the psychology of romantic love, says that basic similarities coupled with complementary differences form the basis of attraction of a man and a woman. That means when you meet someone whose manner of being in the world is similar to yours, there is a shock of instant recognition. This initial recognition could then become the base for forming the structure that supports the relationship. [22]

However, since no two human beings are the same, the process of development varies from individual to individual. For instance, one person may develop verbal and intellectual skills while another may excel in creativity. Or one person may be oriented toward work and achievements while the other is concerned with nurturing relationships.

Branden observes that people are more likely to fall in love with others with whom they experience both basic similarities and complementary differences. Of course, not all differences between people are complementary. You may have had to relate to people whose thinking about time management, work habits, and moral values were completely alien to you. Imagine being in an intimate relationship with any such person; the mental irritation could prove unbearable. [23]

When a man and a woman experience their differences as complementary, they enjoy a feeling of stimulation and excitement knowing such differences can bring out qualities that might have otherwise gone untapped.

Rhythm and energy

Two people can also have different biological rhythm and energy levels. Biological studies have discovered that humans possess an inherent biological rhythm. This is included in their genetic make up and can be modified only slightly within the first two or three years of life, but almost never thereafter. [24]

Biologists have linked this phenomenon to speech patterns, body movements, and emotional response and, to some extent, to temperament. Psychologists noted that people who meet and are on the verge of falling in love sometimes experience a subtle, somewhat mysterious friction between them. They are unable to explain it, except by a strange feeling of being "out of sync" with each other. They sometimes feel irritated and cannot account for their feelings.

Nathaniel Branden says the barrier to an unsuccessful union may be due to incompatible differences in biological rhythm and inherent energy levels. Perhaps you have had this experience. You are trying to carry on a conversation with someone. You find it takes a while for your words to sink in. You wait for a response but it is slow in coming. You feel irritated and anxious, sometimes to the point of frustration. Now think about the person with whom you are speaking. He/she likely feels pressured seeing the frustrated look on your face and hearing the anxiety in your voice.

Now imagine two people who meet, fall in love, and get married but were not aware of this biological incompatibility factor. Naturally, this produces a state of anxiety. The person who is naturally faster feels chronically impatient, while the slower person constantly feels pressured. It's easy to see why constant bickering could result in such a relationship.

Not understanding this phenomenon causes couples to invent reasons for their quarrels. Each partner will look for faults in the other and will name these alleged faults as reasons why a break up finally results. This does not mean people who vary in rhythm and energy levels cannot fall in love. In fact, men and women have fallen in love in spite of this area of conflict. They have overcome it when there are enough positive elements surrounding the relationship. More often than not, however, this is not the case; the difficulties are so overwhelming that the couple has no other choice but to end the relationship. The sad part is that many couples separate without understanding the true reasons for the breakup.

Relationship history

Whenever you meet people in their 20s, 30s, or 40s who are unmarried, you undoubtedly want to know why. If you later discover they have been married before, you become anxious to learn the reasons why the previous relationships ended.

Knowing a person's relationship track record can provide valuable information about how he/she will perform in a new relationship. Some people may be hesitant to openly discuss previous relationships while others will say even more than the listener wants to hear.

If you find that a man is shy or reluctant to speak about past relationships, be patient, give him time to warm up to you. One good way to do this is to say something like this, "You can imagine how I felt after going with my fiancé for over four years. We did everything together. I couldn't imagine a life with anyone else but him. I was devastated when it finally became clear we were just not meant for each other. It took me almost a year to finally accept the fact that I was alone. It was tough, but I am over it now. How did your relationship end?"

However you obtain the information, it is vital that you listen to as many details as possible. You will need all the facts to be able to decide whether you want to take a chance with him. It is possible he made a poor decision in the selection of a mate or perhaps he lacks what it takes to maintain a loving relationship. As he speaks, you will be able to better understand his attitude toward relationships and toward women in general. Ask questions; focus on areas important to you. Make mental notes and remember to write entries in your dating diary as soon and as often as possible.

Why did your last relationship failed?

He might be truthful in his account of what happened, but remember that it is natural for most people to slant a story in their own favor. Keep in mind that you are hearing the story from his point of view. For example, he may say that he and his partner fought mainly because she believed he was not supportive of her career. He goes on to explain that he did have interest in her work, but that was the only thing they talked about. He grew tired of listening to daily reports of her work activities. By asking the right questions, he may discover he is truly uncomfortable with a mate who has a career because he believes a woman's job is to take care of her family.

Was there another woman?

If a man is comfortable seeing another woman while he is in a committed relationship, he may not be the man for you. If he tells you it's not his normal pattern of behavior, watch out. He may repeat the pattern when he is in a relationship with you. You may want to rationalize, "Maybe his last girlfriend was to blame, maybe she deserved it." But even if this were true, an honorable man would break off the old relationship before he embarks on a new one.

Has he ever been married?

You know the type: attractive, financially comfortable, and in hot pursuit by half the available women in the city. Such a man knows how to pamper a woman; best restaurants, lavish gifts, extraordinary manners. Yet he is about 40 years old and has never been married. He claims he will settle down when he finds the right woman.

Yes, there is a possibility you could be the exception and it is a great challenge to succeed where all others have failed. But is it really worth it? Why spend your time hoping he will propose to you some day when hundreds of eligible men are ready to propose to you right now?

If a man has not been able to find a suitable partner in all these years, it is unlikely that you will be the one. The longer he remains single, the more unlikely he is to find a mate with whom he is compatible. If he wants to be your casual friend, that's fine as long as you remember not to expect any more than casual friendships.

Sexual chemistry

Is there a strong sexual attraction between you and your partner?

What is sexual chemistry?

Sexual chemistry is difficult to define. Think of it as something that clicks between two people; you either have it or you don't. How many times have you heard from friends how gorgeous a man looks? When you finally meet him, you realize that as gorgeous as he might appear to others, he does nothing for you. That is because your subconscious mind does not detect the presence of what it needs to establish that physical connection.

Sexual chemistry can be compared to the process that takes place in the combustion chamber of an automobile engine. With precise timing, a spark is introduced into the right mixture of air and gasoline. That produces combustion and, as if by magic, all systems begin to function.

In a similar way, the vibrations from your body mesh with the vibrations of another person, which happens to be on the same wave length as you are to produce energy called sexuality.

When sexual energy is present, it produces mutual physical attraction, referred to as sexual chemistry. This erotic connection strengthens your emotional ties with your lover, and goes a long way in providing a powerful bond in a loving relationship.

Sexual compatibility plays a great part in a loving relationship between two people, yet countless numbers of people spend years in sexually unfulfilling marriages. One woman I know, married and living with her husband, has not had sexual relations for the past five years. Of course, this is an extreme case but many situations of sexless relationships exist today, according to a team of researchers at Georgia State University. [25] Some people who find themselves in sexual unhappy relationships usually justify their position with a variety of excuses. Jennifer, 37, lived with her three children after her divorce from her husband three years ago. She met Andrew, a 53-year-old bus driver, and after eight months of dating, they decided to live together and planned to marry some time in the future.

"My husband and I had a great sexual relationship but our marriage was not going well; we spent most of our time fighting. I've had the feeling that he was cheating on me, but he always denied it. When I discovered that he was having an affair with one of my friends, I decided that I could not live with him anymore. Now my life with Andrew is very peaceful, we hardly have arguments, and he treats my children as if they were his own. He is a good provider; so what if I don't feel sexually attracted to him. We have sex once in a while but I don't look forward to it like I did when I was with my husband. There are so many other things in life that we enjoy, I don't even think about sex."

Jennifer's story is common, but I'm sure you've heard others.

I believe that sex is highly overrated anyway.

She is such a good wife and mother, so I guess I can live without the sex.

Most people are less interested in sex as they get older, so it's no big deal that we don't have sex like we used to.

The importance of sexual attraction

Studies have shown that, in the absence of sexual satisfaction, a relationship usually stands on shaky ground. Respect for your partner, commitment to your relationship, love and consideration for your mate, although vital to a successful relationship, cannot replace satisfying sex.

For your relationship to flourish, some form of sexual activity must exist between you and your partner. Why? Because sex provides a special connection between two people that binds them together in a primal and physical way, notes Patrick Zukeran, research associate for Probe Ministries. [26] This connection is difficult to put in words, but you will understand it better when you have a sexual connection with someone.

Sexual chemistry works well when accompanied by a loving relationship, but it can and often does exist between two people who are not emotionally committed to each other. For this reason, be careful not to mistake sexual attraction for love; an error that has been responsible for numerous failed relationships. You have no doubt heard people say, "I will know it immediately when I meet the partner who is right for me." Yes, people can be misled by a strong physical connection, believing that it is love at first sight. And, yes, you have to know him/her before you can fall in love.

Chapter Seven

Do I love you because
I need you or do I need you
because I love you?
—Erich Fromm

What is love?

What does it mean when you say to someone "I love you?" There are many answers and interpretations to this question, but when asked, the majority of people said that love is something they feel but cannot explain in words. People who genuinely feel they have fallen in love report a warm fuzzy inner feeling, sometimes giddiness. And, according to Psychiatrist Donatella Marazziti, of the University of Pisa, "Falling madly in love may really make you mentally ill." [27]

People constantly ask, "How will I know when it's true love? How can I be certain if and when it hits me?" In an attempt to provide answers to these questions, our interviewers asked dozens of people who said that they had experienced the feeling of falling in love. Their answers and my own experiences over the years led me to the following conclusions:

People who fall in love recognize a strong force that draws them close to each other. Sometimes this force can be a strong physical attraction, which psychologists say is an important ingredient in romantic love. Sometimes, it's more than that. And modern research suggests that over the centuries, our bodies have developed processes to ensure we fall in love with the opposite sex, according to anthropologist Helen E. Fisher PhD.[28]

A Biological explanation

An individual may begin a sexual liaison with a partner sometimes purely for sexual pleasure, then discover that he/she feels a strong attraction for the partner. In many such instances, one or both parties may mistake this attraction for lasting love. Many of us are no doubt aware of how costly such mistakes can be. Helen E. Fisher, PhD., in her study "Brains Do It: Lust, Attraction and Attachment," says that this attraction can be explained biologically. She discovered that, after orgasm, there is a rise in levels of the hormones vasopressin in men and oxytocin in women. These hormones are known for their attachment-causing properties, which led Fisher to conclude that the presence of these chemicals in the body is responsible for the closeness many couples experience after sexual intercourse.

A study referenced in an article in *Cerebrum, a Dana Forum on Brain Science* further explains three systems associated with mating, reproduction, and parenting. These systems are called Lust, Attraction, and Attachment.

Lust: This is nature's way of ensuring that a male and a female are sufficiently motivated to engage in the mating process.

Attraction: This system keeps both parties passionately focused on each other until insemination is accomplished. Fisher sees the evolution of the attraction system as a way for individuals to select and maintain focus on the most eligible partner. Individuals thought to be genetically superior were, and still are, considered to be more desirable as mating partners.

Attachment: This emotion system (termed 'compassionate love') has evolved to ensure that offspring are nurtured and cared for. The increased levels of the hormones vasopressin and oxytocin mentioned above indicates nature's intention to keep parents together for joint parenting, at least until offspring are able to care for themselves. It is interesting to note that the report suggests Lust and Attraction does not always go hand in hand. When men and women were injected with testosterone- a hormone known to increase sexual desire-their sex drives did increase but they did not fall in love.

In this report, Fisher also refers to studies carried out by D. Marazzitti and associates who concluded that falling in love is associated with low levels of the hormone serotonin. [29] But according to Marazzitti, this chemical balance in humans does not remain constant, confirming that passionate attraction does not last forever. She noted that, when tested after a while, the levels of serotonin in the bodies of infatuated men and women change, returning to similar levels observed in subjects who had not fallen in love. Marazzitti and her team established the duration of infatuation between lovers from a period of 12 to 18 months.

This research is important because it explains how our biological system works in concert with our emotional processes. Whenever we find a suitable partner, we can then rely on our chemical and biological systems to assist us in achieving our emotional goals. And when we find that our partners seem less attracted to us, it does not necessarily mean they have fallen out of love with us. It may simply mean their biological processes are performing normally.

People say they are seeking their soul mates-the one person who shares how they view life itself, their most important values, and the driving force that moves them. Nathaniel Branden, PhD, says "When we meet another person, we sense how that individual experiences him or herself. We sense the level of that person's excitement or the lack of it. Our instant attraction or non attraction is automatic because our bodies and emotions respond faster than thought can take shape in words."

Each person is a unique being. What we sense at this moment is that the other person possesses what it takes to complement our lives. We sense that a union with such a person can bring new possibilities, which can make our existence richer. This is not to say this newfound person is the only one who can be right. There may be others. For this reason, it has been concluded that, for each person, more than one soul mate exists, according to Andrea N. Jones of *Youth Outlook,* a newspaper published by *Pacific News Service.* [30]

This instant identification of compatibility can take place on your first contact or later as you become more familiar with each other. And because the events are too rapid for your logical thought processes, all you know is that you sense this instant connection but cannot explain reasons for it.

Later on, as you become more familiar with your partner and begin to understand his/her way of being, reactions to, and expression of emotions etc., you may be able to identify similarities, thus explaining the initial mutual attraction. It's true that the initial attraction can bring couples together, but love goes much deeper than that.

Falling in love is not being in love

Many people meet, are attracted to each other, and fall in love but do not live happily ever after. Why? Because most of them are confused by the meaning of love.

Let's look at an explanation of love; there are many, but this one seems most accurate. When you love someone, you value that person highly-so highly that you have made a choice to offer your resources to nurture the one you love. You have also chosen to place her/his well-being and development as your highest priority. Yes, it is a choice, and to make a choice, you need information. Information gathering requires time. For this reason, there is no such thing as true love at first sight.

However, to offer yourself in this case does not mean to sacrifice or deprive you of resources. Most people relate "giving" to "relieving oneself of resources." But psychologists familiar with human behavior observe that "giving love" has a different meaning. When you give love, you experience strength, joy, and aliveness.

Therefore, those who give of themselves are bestowing on another the most precious gift they have to offer: their joys, their understandings, and their love for life. To them, these things are more valuable than money, yet they are willing to give them freely. Then something wonderful happens. By giving, they enrich another's life with the same joy, aliveness, and understanding that is a part of them. When all of these good things enhance the other person's life, that person radiates those feelings, giving birth to a new joy, which can be shared by them both. So by giving love, people automatically receive love in return, even though they do not give it with this intention.

"The greatest thing we ever learn is
to love and give love in return."
—Nat King Cole, Miles Davis

Why do we need love?

From the moment we are born and even before, nature provides us with the security of a mother's love. Without that love, it would be difficult to survive. A mother's love is synonymous with care, protection, and nurturing. Our relationship with "mother" represented our first perception of love. As we progressed in life, we learned that love means taking care of our own well-being.

It has been said that mother's love is the purest form of love that exists, love that requires nothing more than being alive. Some people continue to seek this kind of love in other relationships even after they have grown up and become adults. A friend of mine said his mother once told him if he could find a woman who can tolerate his faults the way that she (his mother) can, he should marry her immediately. My friend is nearly 50 years old and not yet married.

Mother's love, by its very nature, is one-sided; one party gives while the other receives. In romantic and other forms of love, equality rules; both parties mutually share giving and receiving. Relationships other than those between mother and child, which are built on inequality, stand little chance of survival. Of course we all know of relationships of exploitation where both parties are dependent on each other; the "exploiter" needs someone to exploit and the "dependent" one needs to be exploited. Such relationships function as long as such mutual dependency continues to exist.

Companionship

In addition to the basic need for existence, humans have always exhibited the need for companionship. People need at least one person with whom to share intimacy and their most important values of life.

People also need to find things, we value, things which give us pleasure, which we can love, which give us a reason for living. We have seen that people who find themselves alone due to the loss of loved ones and simply choose to be alone may keep a pet or a plant in their home. Remember, a healthy plant will not only bring life into your space, but also absorb toxins in the air.

Need for appreciation

In the year 2001, a CNN opinion poll named U.S. President George Bush "the most loved man in America." [31] Bush has gained the approval of the American people for his effort in the war against terrorism. American people have recognized Bush and shown appreciation for his personal dedication and sacrifice. But why does he do it? Why does a man who has obviously had many great successes in his life continue to strive for even higher levels of excellence?

Many will say such men are driven by the need for power. This may be true, but psychological studies have linked the need for power with the desire to be loved. Many winners of the Academy awards for Motion Pictures have said their struggles are fueled by their need to be loved and appreciated by their fans. It is a fact that people who have achieved great levels of success in their lives are usually admired, respected, and loved for their achievements. [32]

Is love forever?

Debbie, 33, a credit collector for a shipping company, recently ended a three-year relationship. "From the moment I met Jerry, I knew he was right for me but experience taught me to proceed cautiously. After about four months of dating, I decided my first impressions were right; he was everything I always wanted in a man. We had three happy years together and Jerry repeatedly told me how contented he was to have found someone with whom he could share his life.

"We did everything together, took business courses, went on vacations, even saw the same movies. Living together was comfortable, but for some reason the thought of marriage never appealed to me. We had talked about having a family some day, but whenever Jerry brought up the subject, I felt I was not yet ready. Jerry wanted to take our relationship to the next level but I felt comfortable with the way things were. For the first time in our relationship, it dawned on me that my relationship with Jerry may not be forever. This frightened me because I truly loved him but I knew that I was not ready to get married to him.

"When I finally realized Jerry really wanted marriage, a strange thing happened. I began to feel uneasy with our relationship. Things were not like before; I lost some of my excitement and desire to be with him. It's as if I was inconsiderate to him after he had been so good to me. I felt like I did not deserve to be with him. We finally agreed to go our separate ways, and even though I miss him, I feel that somewhere along the way the love I had for him was lost.

"It's been four years since Jerry and I ended our relationship, and I am still trying to understand what happened between us. I've been seeing other guys, but so far I have not experienced the closeness I had with Jerry. My friends tell me I'm not yet ready to settle down with anyone, and maybe there're right. In my relationship with Jerry I felt free to be myself. We lived together like buddies without feeling tied down to each other, (at least that's the way I felt). When he became serious about marriage, I no longer saw him as a buddy, but as someone who was going to tie me down. I just got scared."

Do you believe this relationship was one of true love? Some may say it was a mistake because Debbie and Jerry were not truly compatible and should not have been together in the first place.

In my opinion, this relationship was successful because both participants enjoyed three fulfilling years of their lives together. Someone once said if you can have one moment of true happiness in your life, grab it because true happiness is not easy to find.

Love is a living entity; if it stands still, it could die. To be alive means to move forward and go where life's journey takes you. Love may die only to be reborn again in a different form. Perhaps both Jerry and Debbie will move on to find love in different places, but they will always cherish the love they once shared with each other.

Seven ways to tell if he/she truly loves you

A woman once asked, "Ok, I heard all the love stories of people being on cloud nine or feel surrounded by fresh roses that bloom only for them. But after all this, how do I know that he truly loves me? How could I be sure after being together for more than a year that his love is real?"

Here are seven ways to tell if he/she loves you.

1. You know that your partner truly loves you when he/she seems interested in every last detail about you. When he/she really wants to know how your day was, how you feel, and what you are thinking. Whenever you have something to say, you can tell by the look on his/her face that he/she is truly listening.

2. When things go wrong (for example, a misunderstanding or disagreement), you know that no matter how mad he/she gets, deep inside, your relationship is not in jeopardy. Ian, a stockbroker, said, "My wife sometimes gets on my nerves and many times I just can't hide my anger. But strangely I never feel any resentment or ill feelings toward her."

3. Some people, no matter how hard they try, find it difficult to openly express their emotions. Even if this is true with your partner, you can tell if he/she loves you by the way he/she reacts to your touch. For example, if you were to hug your mate, you will feel the love that exists between you. When you feel it, you will know it.

4. You know that your partner loves you when the people

around you clearly notice how special he/she treats you in public. Mary, 37, a travel agent said her friends tell her they know Jim adores her by the way his face lights up whenever she is around.

5. You know that your partner loves you when he/she wants to share everything with you. I once asked my wife, "Do you want to fatten me? Why is it that every time you put something in your mouth, you offer some to me? She replied, "Because I am enjoying it and I want you to feel exactly the way I am feeling."

6. You know that she/he loves you when you can confidently say, "I trust you." You feel sure that, no matter what, your partner will not betray you.

If you listen carefully to the words used during a wedding ceremony, you will observe that an important word is missing. That word is trust. By Webster's definition, "trust is an assured reliance on the integrity and reliability of another." You will hear the words "love, respect, and comfort, cherish and honor," but strangely, not the word "trust." Trust is a vitally important ingredient in any loving relationship, but does not come easily or immediately. No matter how much you may love someone even after marriage, trust has to be tested and proven over time.

7. Of all the women I've interviewed on the subject of love, Maxine, a 42-year old housewife and mother, struck me as being the most certain of her relationship. She said. "When I started seeing Herb over two years ago, I was going through a series of hardships in my life. I had recently separated from my previous husband. After eight years of marriage, he took off, leaving me with three kids and very little money. At that time, I was definitely not in the mental state to start a new relationship with anyone. But Herb persisted. It was a trying period for both of us because I was very unreceptive to him. At times, I even wondered why he would want to continue to waste his time with me;

I was extremely difficult to get along with.

"In spite of all this, however, Herb and I formalized our relationship together after dating for about two years. After we had lived together for more than a year and everything worked out fine, I asked him why he had been so persistent with me. Herb explained that even though I seemed impossible to live with, he knew that deep inside I was a kind, loving, sincere, and, in many ways a very special person.

"I guess I always knew, but at that particular moment, it struck me that Herb knew my heart. I am sure that he truly loves me because he had taken the time to know the real me."

A chilling experience

Not everyone gets the opportunity to positively confirm feelings of true love for someone. I had this opportunity through a chilling experience, and though I would never want to repeat it, I am grateful for this particular incident that tested our love.

My wife Diomira and I were on a mineral exploration trip on a river near Venezuela in South America. It was a mountainous area accessible only by river. Because of the rocky terrain and numerous waterfalls, we could not reach our destination in one boat trip.

With the assistance of three helpers, we traveled as far as we could in a small boat powered by an outboard engine. We then removed the outboard engine and secured the boat at the bottom of a waterfall. We had to carry the outboard around a mountain pass on foot. The plan was to attach the engine to another boat, which was kept at a launching point higher up the mountain, and continue the trip in that boat.

It took about two hours to walk around the mountain. By the time we reached the other boat, everyone was exhausted. In hindsight, it would have been wise to rest for at least a half an hour. But it was getting late and we still faced a two-hour boat ride to reach the camp where we'd spend the night.

It is important to understand the danger that surrounded us. Remember, we had just bypassed several rocky sections of the river to arrive at this point, which was the beginning of the waterfalls. We got in to the second boat about 100 yards from where the actual falls began. This part of the falls has two drops, one about 30 feet and the other 20 feet. The river then levels off into a pool about 80 to 100 feet deep. We knew there would be a strong current in this area.

However, this was not the first time we made this journey, so we felt familiar with the steps needed to keep the boat clear of the current. But we got too comfortable. We even left our life jackets in the first boat because we were too lazy to carry them.

One of the attendants attached the outboard to the boat and we were ready to go. He started the motor and pushed off. We learned afterwards that carrying the outboard for so long caused the gasoline in the carburetor to dry up. This meant the engine had to be primed before taking off to ensure a steady gasoline flow. But this step had been bypassed.

As a consequence, the engine stopped when we were in the centre of the river. Our boat immediately began to drift backward toward the waterfalls. At first, the attendant did not lose his cool. He pulled the starting cord and tried to prime the engine so gasoline could reach the carburetor. But it did not work and we were clearly going down. So he and two others abandoned the boat and swam 80 yards to the riverbank.

The boat was now less than a minute away from the first drop, and Diomira and I were still in it. I saw the fear in her eyes. We were both wearing twelve-inch high, open-top leather boots.

We knew we could die because, even if we survived the two drops, our boots would fill with water and make it impossible to swim to safety.

In a split second, I decided the boots had to be removed. But there was only time enough to remove either my wife's boots or my own, not both. Diomira, in a state of shock, did not even think about her boots. So I grabbed her legs and dragged them off her feet just before the boat plunged down the drop.

Miraculously, we both came out of the fall alive with only one broken bone. Clearly, removing her boots saved Diomira's life because she was able to swim ashore after she was thrown into the deep. Ironically, it turned out that my boots saved me from getting caught in a cave below the falls where I would have certainly drowned.

The gods were watching over us that day.

Can you find true love the second time around?

Entering a remarriage is like walking onto a movie set long after the film has begun.
—Susan Kelly

The Census Bureau of the United States reported that more than 40% of all marriages are **remarriages** for at least one of the parties involved and predicted that 75% of all divorced people would remarry. Over the years, these figures have remained constant despite the numerous statistics showing that remarried people divorce at the same or even (higher) rate as people in first-time marriages. It would seem that despite the statistics, people seem to prefer being attached to someone instead of being single. [33]

Many second timers say they found in their second marriages some of the things missing in their first. This is not surprising since many marriage experts say it is unreasonable to expect young people entering marriage for the first time to possess all the tools needed for a successful marriage partnership. Perhaps people acquire more wisdom when selecting a truly compatible partner, or better problem-solving skills, from the knowledge and insights we gain from our previous experiences.

To those who would like to give romance another chance, or say you meet someone who wants to start over with you, some of the challenges you are likely to face are described below.

Your priorities may change in a second marriage

Some things that were important in your first marriage might have less significance in a subsequent marriage. For example, physical appearance may have been a motivating factor when you selected your first partner. In a second marriage, you may choose someone who can assist you in achieving financial security and a more comfortable life.

A man who has gone through a marital relationship before may have different priorities on his second attempt. If he already has children, he may not have the desire to have more children with a new partner. In first marriages, the differences between husband and wife are usually two years. However, when a divorced man marries a single woman, there is usually a greater gap in age differences. Having gone through the process already, a man may decide…

- He is too advanced in age to be a proper father to infants and small children.
- His financial situation does not allow for the support of himself, his previous children, and a new family with children.
- The responsibilities and sacrifices of having children far outweigh the rewards.

Of course the man should communicate his decisions to the woman beforehand. A woman who has never had children might seriously resent the idea of being denied the right to do so.

What about women who are mothers already?

Some women who have already had their children may marry a man who wants children of his own. Depending on the circumstances, a woman may be willing to satisfy the wishes of her new husband. If she truly loves him, she may actually want to produce a child from the union. But many divorced mothers said they had children in their new marriages because their husbands wanted to have them.

From the information gathered from divorced mothers, it would seem that the majority would prefer not to have children in a second or subsequent marriage. Why? One might be tempted to say that a woman who has experienced the effort and sacrifices involved in raising a family would prefer not to do it again. Although this may be true in some cases, psychological studies point to other reasons. [34]

A woman in the process of selecting a husband or long-term partner for the first time sees her new mate as her knight in shining armor. In him, she pictures a bright future for herself. She sees marriage, social recognition, the excitement and adventure of building a life together, and perhaps the possibilities of starting a family. In return for the life she desires, she gives to the union what is most precious to her: her love, her heart, and her soul.

Let's assume her marital relationship is successful, she accomplishes what she desired, and enjoys a happy life. Suppose for some reason, be it death or divorce, the woman becomes separated from her partner. Can she love a new mate with the similar passion she loved her first partner?

Most women who were once married but are now separated said, they would find it hard to trust another man the way they trusted their first husbands. No doubt some women were referring to a betrayal or disappointment they may have experienced with their previous husbands. But even women whose husbands had died also did not feel they could give the same love to another man that they gave to their first. Perhaps there is some truth to the old saying, "First love never dies." But it's more than that. Some women believe that the part of themselves (their youth, innocence, enthusiasm, and trust) they gave to their first relationship is no longer available to give to anyone else.

It is not difficult to understand why a woman might feel this way. She has already achieved what she may have considered her life-long desires: a fine husband, social respect, the security of companionship, and a happy family life. She has completed this phase and does not need to repeat it. Her teenage fantasies have been fulfilled and she is ready to move on. Her new goals may include raising her children, who have likely become the number-one priority in her life. So if she should decide to seek a new mate, her reasons and expectations of a new relationship may be different from those she set for her first marriage.

No doubt she would still need love and companionship, but her vision of love may not be the same as when she loved for the first time. Her prince has come and gone but the memories he created can last a lifetime. There will always be a place in her heart reserved for him, more so when children are involved. This is not to say she cannot find happiness with another man; more than likely she would. But now she is probably wiser and better equipped to choose someone who can suit her needs better as she gets older. Her choices may be determined more by logic rather than by instinct, but sometimes there are other complications.

Feeling left out

Even in a second or third marriage, most men seek a soul mate, a partner with whom they can intimately share most aspects of their lives. However, a woman who has already had a relationship as described above may wish to keep certain parts of her life separate from her new partner. This sometimes causes both the man and the woman to experience a lack of intimacy in the relationship.

Kenny, a 38 year-old divorced real estate agent, is having doubts about marrying Shirley, an attractive 39-year-old divorced mother of three. Kenny feels that even though Shirley says she loves him and he believes that she does, he feels he is not getting 100% of her love.

"I know something is missing but I can't put my finger on it. I adore Shirley and we are even discussing marriage. I get along great with the kids, and I believe we can make a happy family together. Financially we are okay. I make a good income and she had a modest settlement from her previous marriage. We share a lot of time together but, for some reason, Shirley wants to exclude me from certain aspects of her life. For example, she likes to take the kids on vacation by herself because she says she needs to spend time alone with them. I know that people need their personal time and space, but I feel that I am being left out from too much of her life."

Mature people would not expect to be joined at the hip with their partners, but would want to be included in important activities in their partner's lives. Shirley may have considered her children of such great value to her that she did not want to share them, even with the man she loved.

A woman who has been married before may protect herself from repeating her mistakes by having a long list of requirements that a new partner must satisfy before she gets seriously involved with him. If she sets her standards too high, then it may take her longer to find someone suitable. But setting high standards might be a way she subconsciously protects herself from getting involved with a new partner. She may genuinely wish to wait a while especially if she has a family and has gained some level of financial independence from a career and a previous marriage.

Four reasons why a woman may not be ready to love again

1. A feeling of guilt

Some women may feel they were responsible for the break up when their relationships ended. She may reason, for example, that if she did not make so many demands on her partner, or if she had been less critical about his parents, maybe they would still be together. Such a woman may wish to remain single for a while in the hope that her partner might return. Even if he dies, she may blame herself. "Maybe if I had taken better care of him, he might still be around today." In cases when the husband dies, the woman might believe she would be betraying her dead husband if she was to love another man. She may truly feel that if she finds happiness again, it would mean she really did not love her former husband. When you truly love someone, you always want the best for him/her. Even in death, a loving husband would want his wife to find happiness and move on with her life.

According to John Gray, author of *Men are from Mars, Women are from Venus*, we feel pain when we lose a loved one because we are resisting the loss. Once we find a way to accept our loss, the pain goes away. And even if the pain goes away, the feeling we have for our loved ones stays with us.

2. Holding out for the right partner

When a man or woman has unresolved feelings from a past relationship, he/she tends to hold out for the perfect partner. Instead of working with what's available when seeking a partner, he/she may continue to have unrealistic expectations, which can prove difficult if not impossible to achieve.

If you were involved in a marital relationship before, you may tend to judge future relationships by the standards of your previous ones. Even when a relationship ends in divorce, you may glorify the good qualities of your "ex" and unconsciously seek them in your new partners. If a partner should fall short, you may find him unsuitable. But good qualities come in all shapes and sizes, and someone who might seem unsuitable at first could turn out to be quite fascinating as you get closer. You have to give love a chance.

Some women may sit back expecting an earth-shaking experience as a signal of being ready to fall in love again. She may believe the right man will spark in her a renewed passion for living. If she does not experience a burning desire for romance soon after she meets him, then she believes he cannot be the right person for her.

People who depend on others to ignite their passion for living are usually disappointed. You can attract someone more quickly when you yourself possess the desire for romance. No one can turn you on if you are not ready to be turned on. In any case, you should be on your guard if you are immediately attracted to someone. Instant attraction is a good beginning but should not be mistaken for lasting love. Lasting love requires time, communication, and investigation.

3. First loyalty to children

When a woman becomes a single parent because of death or divorce, she may decide, "Now more than ever my children need me." She may try to compensate for the lack of a father by being both mother and father to her children. Most mothers are already 100% committed to their children, but in the absence of a father, a mother may make even greater sacrifices for their well-being.

It is easy for a mother to suppress her needs for love and intimacy while focusing on being a parent. However, this is neither good for the mother nor the children. Children can feel the burden of their mother's sacrifice for them and, in return, feel responsible for the mother's happiness. But adults have needs that cannot be satisfied by children. Imagine the psychological pain children suffer when they are unable to make their mother happy. I know of a seven-year-old girl who developed a stomach ulcer because of this. She was diagnosed as being under tremendous psychological stress due to family problems.

A friend of mine who is raising two children on her own showed me a letter she found in her five-year-old son's room. It was addressed to his gym schoolteacher. With some grammatical corrections and a change of names, it read: *"Dear Mr..... I want you to come to our house and be a friend for my mom. My father lives at my grandma's house so my mom has to sleep by herself. My mom works very hard to do everything for us. My mom is a nice lady. You are a very nice man and my Mom will like you. Danny."*

Women who place the needs of their children as their highest priority, even before their own needs, subconsciously push love away by being overly protective with their children. `Some women put their love life on hold for years to avoid introducing another man into their children's lives. They believe that by sacrificing their own happiness, they can reassure their children that their mother will always be there for them. Children do become jealous when their parents get involved with a new lover, and sometimes with good reason. Some women pay less attention to their children when they fall in love with a new partner. However, I believe this is not a good reason for a mother to avoid love.

Experts recommend parents should get involved in a new relationship as soon as it's convenient, if they so desire. The presence of a new partner in their parent's lives forces children to face the reality that their father or mother is no longer around. When a child accepts the loss of a parent, she will be better prepared to accept the changes that may take place in her family. The mother can then concentrate on helping her children overcome their jealousy. [35]

Sometimes a mother tries to protect her children from feeling jealous by downplaying her show of affection for her new partner. Judi, a 35-year-old divorced mother of two, said, "I told my boyfriend that I will not be ready to marry him until my children are old enough to be on their own. We have a good relationship but I would never let him sleep over when the boys are around. By now, he knows he is not allowed to be affectionate with me in the presence of my children. As far as the children are concerned, he is a good friend and that's all."

Even when a woman remarries or moves in with a new partner, she may try to mislead her children into believing she is not madly in love with her new partner. Some mothers do this to reassure their children they can still count on all her love. Children can sometimes fear their mother's love may be taken away from them and given to her new partner. Trying to protect your children in this way may seem like a good idea, but could cause undue strain on your relationship with your mate. Even though your partner may understand your objective, he may still feel uncomfortable with your actions.

Such actions can also confuse younger children who may wonder, "Why, is he living with us if Mom is not in love with him?"

It is preferable for a parent to let children know the new partner is very important to him/her. But even though they love each other, it has nothing to do with the love that the parents share with the children. Parents need to assure children that no one can take such love away from them.

Most children would love to have single parents all to themselves, but would welcome someone new when they sense that the newcomer makes mommy or daddy happy.

4. Too much independence

If, after a loss, a woman succeeds in suppressing her needs for romantic love for a considerable length of time, she may wonder if she really needs a man. Her determination to succeed in taking care of herself and her children may have driven her to become overly self-sufficient. She may have learned to live without love, having discovered, for example, that furthering her career can be just as fulfilling.

A recent article in the *New York Times* referred to a large number of eligible adult women spread across the U.S. These women have gained success in their careers and/or in business and are financially secure. The question is, however, are they truly eligible?

The longer a woman manages to live her life without a partner, the more difficult it may become for her to find love. Sometimes her resolve to make it on her own drives her further away from men. She may actually lose her desire to fully enjoy life and fall in love. These women should not be confused with those who have given up on men, or those who feel that all men are no good. I am referring to those who genuinely believe they can make it on their own and would like to live that way.

When a woman reaches this level of self-confidence, she usually sends clear signals of her independence. She may not do so consciously, but she may unknowingly convey the "I am strong, self-sufficient, do not need assistance" stance.

Most men are attracted to women when they believe they can make a significant difference in the woman's life. A woman who disconnects from her feelings may send a clear signal that she is not receptive to what a man may offer. When a man has a choice, he may ignore such a woman and move on to a more receptive one. Of course, there is always the man who thrives on the challenge of convincing a woman that he is the best thing that could ever happen to her.

The downside to all this becomes evident when a woman who has succeeded in what she has set out to achieve suddenly feels the need for companionship. I have spoken to several of these women who said they have tried without success to find a compatible partner.

Picture a woman financially self-sufficient who has lived without a companion for a number of years and has become set in her ways. To her, it may be extremely difficult to share intimacy with anyone. A great many of these women find themselves in the company of men who are clearly not compatible with them.

Phyllis, a 47-year-old air traffic controller, has been divorced for 12 years. "Sometimes I believe I am setting my standards too high, but even when I try to compromise, it doesn't work out. Take for instance this new boyfriend I've been seeing. We were planning a vacation; a well-deserved one for me. I wanted to get away for a whole month. First the question of whether or not he can afford such a trip came up. Then there was the problem of not having free time because he can't get leave from his job. In the end, we could not make the trip."

It's a catch 22. The men who may be suitable to your taste

may not be attracted to you, and the men who are attracted to you are not compatible with you. Some women may find they have even priced themselves clear out of the market.

Pre-nup or no pre-nup

A problem that is becoming more common in the United States, especially in remarriages, is the protection of assets. A man or woman who possesses a substantial financial portfolio may want to protect such assets in case the marriage or relationship fails. A prenuptial agreement provides such protection. This is a signed agreement between couples generally limiting the value of assets to be divided if a separation occurs.

Many people see a prenuptial agreement as a lack of trust. "If you love me, why do you think that our relationship will not last?" Of course, we all know the answer to this question, especially when it works out better for the person with the smaller assets. For example, judges in court have been known to give preference to children of a first marriage over those of a second marriage. So even as a second wife, you may not be well protected if you do not have a prior agreement.

You may think all this talk about prenuptial agreements applies to rich people only. But consider this: Ron ran a small business in Atlanta. At 57 years old and divorced, he was earning just enough to support himself but nothing more. He got together with Agnes, 60, an old girlfriend who had done well for herself, now divorced and living in California. After several discussions, they decided that Ron would give up his business and move in with Agnes at her home in California. Agnes agreed to provide the finances for Ron to start a new business there. Everything went well and they got married.

After four years of living together, it became clear they could not continue their relationship. The business had failed and they were fighting like cats and dogs. Ron decided that the only solution was divorce. At least he could make a clean break with a good settlement from her. Or so he thought. Then he found out that all of Agnes's assets were in the names of her children, and that there is nothing much to divide with him. Even the house they lived in was owned by one of her sons. When I spoke to Ron, he was in a state of depression. "She is the most difficult person to live with. Now she blames me for everything. I can't stand it. But what can I do, where can I go? I have given up everything in Atlanta, there is nothing there to return to."

One might immediately say he was naive to walk into a marriage without being aware of such matters, and that Agnes was dishonest to withhold disclosure of the facts. This might be all true, but if Ron had insisted on signing a prenuptial agreement beforehand, he would no doubt have been made aware of the facts.

Compatibility is still key

Whether it is your first, second, or third time around, remember it is important to take the time to determine the level of compatibility between you both. Other areas of compatibility that you need to cover are: religion, habits and patterns, lifestyles, stability, sexual style, ethics, and morals.

Again, only after you truly understand your mate's views, beliefs, and preferences about life, and that these are compatible with your own, can you feel relaxed. Yes, now you can feel confident you have completed a major step that enhances your chances of long-term success in your love union.

Chapter Eight
Now that you are a couple

When is the right time to have sex?

Traditionally, the "double standard" (non marital sex was accepted for males but not for females) was the predominant standard for premarital sexual behavior in American society. [36]

Today, sex in the context of a stable loving relations seems to be the accepted norm for pre-marital relationships. [37]

Whatever the common practice, each individual has his/her own moral values and will be guided by his/her own conscience when it comes to sex.

Past experience, however, has taught people to tread carefully because errors in this area can result in long-term unhappiness. Heartbreak, unwanted pregnancy, and sexually transmitted diseases immediately come to mind.

In the beginning of a relationship, premature sex can mislead you into believing you are in love with your partner, when in fact you only have the hots for him. Some people say they experienced love at first sight when they really felt a strong sexual attraction.

Intense physical attraction for someone may also cause you

to invest emotionally in a relationship, only to be heartbroken after your mate gets his/her fill of sex and moves on.

Timing

Sex is a natural process in a relationship between two people. However, having sex too soon or delaying it too long can affect your chances of marriage or long-term commitment. If you engage in casual sex with a man, it's more than likely he will maintain a casual relationship with you. At the other extreme, if you unreasonably withhold sex after a relationship has progressed to a certain stage of development, a man may believe something is wrong.

How important is sex to a man?

Don't underestimate the importance of sex to a man. You've heard the saying, "The way to a man's heart is through his stomach." From what we know today, it's time to revise that saying. Studies have shown that, to a normal male, sex is second only to self preservation. If a man is not worried about his survival, the next thing he thinks about is sex. [38]

A man considers sex as the greatest gift he can receive from a woman he values highly. He is ready to invest whatever time and effort necessary to win this prize. If a man receives the reward of sex too easily, the value in his mind diminishes. For this reason, you have to be sure your partner has made a considerable emotional investment in you before you begin sexual relations with him.

His morals

If you have properly interviewed your partner in the early stages of your friendship, by now you should be familiar with his moral values. There is little chance of a man marrying a woman who transgresses his moral codes. If, for example, in your discussions with him, it came out indirectly that his moral code for sex is traditional (e.g., he may have told you how shocked he was when he found out his 16-year-old sister was having sex), you have to be extra careful.

Like all men, he will be pushing for sex. You should, however, postpone the act as long as possible even if you are eager to have sex with him.

It is extremely difficult to anticipate a man's sexual preferences and standards even if he tells you. For this reason, I recommend you be as traditional as you can in sex acts whenever you decide to have sex with him. Don't be too innovative. You don't want to shock him. This is one area where you should give the man a chance to be the initiator (in the beginning stages anyway). There is a good reason for this. Even though he is not expecting you to be a virgin, a man would like to feel that his woman has gained most of her sexual experiences from him.

He may also disapprove of certain sex practices. Since you are not aware of his feelings, you may perform certain sexual acts believing that you impress him. He may even enjoy your performance while his subconscious mind resents you for it. If, however, he asks you to engage in non-traditional sex acts, it might be in your interests to try to please him unless you face a serious conflict with your own moral codes.

You must also remember that if you are in a long-term relationship with him and you want him to be monogamous, you will have to satisfy all his sexual needs. If a man does not find the sexual satisfaction he requires at home, he is likely to seek it elsewhere. If you agree to please him in sex acts that are not generally accepted, let him be the one to convince you that such acts are acceptable.

Wrong reasons for having sexual intercourse

- "I felt guilty after going out with him for so long and for not giving him what he wanted." Guilt is not a good reason to sleep with a man.

- "I believed he would not need to see other women if he is getting all he needs from me." If he wants to see other women, no amount of sex from you will stop him.
- "To see if he can satisfy me sexually." Sexual satisfaction depends on many factors, one of which is emotional attachment. In the absence of these factors, you may not experience the satisfaction you expect. You may therefore be misled into believing your partner is incapable of satisfying you.
- "If I can satisfy him sexually, he will fall in love with me." When you jump into bed with a guy too quickly, he may not take you seriously, believing you do the same with every guy you meet. Jacob, 42, a construction worker, said, "It's a guy's thing to push for sex, but if a woman has sex with me too quickly, great, but I want to know how many other guys has she been with this month."
- To find your ideal partner, you may have to date dozens of men. Imagine what it would be like to have sex with each one of them, only to discover later that none was right for you.

Sound reasons for having sexual intercourse

- You are emotionally bonded with your partner and you are mentally ready for sex.
- You have studied your mate long enough to know that he possesses many of the qualities you are looking for in a love partner. Also you are satisfied that you can have a long-term relationship with him.
- You have known him long enough to be sure he is not engaged in any high-risk behavior, homosexual practices, drug use, etc., that can be detrimental to your health.

Delaying sex but keeping his interest

We have spoken about a man's sex drive, but we must not forget that women have equally powerful sexual desires. So while a woman strives to restrain the man sexual advances, she has to exert equal force to restrain her own.

Yes, it is a great sacrifice, but you will have many opportunities to make up for it when you are finally with the one you love. Whatever delaying tactics you may use, however, make sure your man understands you are rejecting sex and not him. In a subtle way, let him know you find him physically desirable but would like to know him better before having sex.

Some women believe that teasing a man increases the chances he will commit to them. Be aware that a man becomes very angry if you arouse his sexual desires without satisfying them. You can entice him by letting him know what's in store for him when the time is right, but don't overdo it.

How to avoid temptation

- Arrange dates filled with activities you both can enjoy. This way, the time passes quickly leaving little time for boredom. In the absence of activity, a man usually pushes for sex.
- When in a man's company, do not drink heavily. Alcohol impairs your judgment, causing you to do things, you may regret later.
- Engage in activities that use up your sexual energy. Putting in some extra effort at your job, and working out at the gym whenever you can, keeps your body and mind occupied.

Your soul mate can be the person
who you can't stand but are in your life
to teach you a powerful lesson.
—Wayne Dyer

Getting closer to each other

After three to six months of dating, you both have decided there is enough mutual attraction to go further in your relationship. Now that you are officially a couple, both you and your lover will become more relaxed with each other. In a relaxed state, people act more naturally. Their time is better spent learning more about each other while getting closer and strengthening the relationship.

Use this opportunity to let your partner know your likes and dislikes. It is better at this stage for him to see you the way you really are because this is the person with whom he will have to live. Some people go out of their way to make a good impression on their mate, but find it difficult to maintain this impression in normal everyday life. Don't say, for example, that you are an ardent lover of opera music when in fact you prefer country and western.

Engage in activities that create memories and at the same time promote learning about each other's preferences for enjoyment. Sometimes a person, you are in love with, can bring out qualities in you that you did not know you had. A friend of mine disliked engaging in games of chance, off-track betting, gambling casinos, etc. After she got married, she and, her husband spent a lot of their free time at gaming establishments. They even traveled to other countries to visit new casinos. She now claims this as her favorite form of enjoyment.

Maintaining standards

Think of the things that attracted your partner to you in the first place. As a woman, you might have been elegantly dressed, outgoing, witty, and self-confident. Maybe you enjoyed an exciting life on your own.

If you drop everything that you're doing to engage in his

activities, making him your center of attention, he may lose some of his desire for you. When you can keep his interest while maintaining your own lifestyle, you are on the right track.

Don't allow him to become complacent

It's common for people to take each other for granted as they become more familiar with each other. A man who might have been otherwise punctual may begin showing up late for dates and forgoing certain courtesies. If your man starts becoming lackadaisical, bring it to his attention immediately. Let him know in a loving but firm way that becoming closer does not eliminate the need for common courtesies.

Nancy, 38, a web-designer, met Joe, 42, a chemical technician, through a matchmaking service. They dated for 11 months before they decided to get engaged. Nancy tells how she was able to put her fiancé back on track.

"While we were dating, Joe was very considerate with me. He would make plans long in advance and always gave me sufficient time to adjust my schedule. After we got engaged, I noticed certain changes in his behavior. He didn't seem to be as organized as he previously was with appointments, and would sometimes show up late for dates. I began to get worried. Could it be that he is losing interest in our relationship?

"I decided to speak to him about it. I said: You know, Joe, I was so impressed with the way you organized things before. You always called ahead and notified me about our plans. Now I notice you don't do that anymore. I like it when you give me advanced notice; it gives me time to prepare, and I am so excited in anticipation of seeing you. Joe assured me he had not lost interest in our relationship, but he did not realize how important making prior arrangements were to me."

Inviting him over for the first time

Whether it is in the first month or later in your relationship, you will want your mate to see where you live. Most men who are considering a stable relationship with a woman look forward to seeing her in her own surroundings. It is, therefore, important to be prepared for his first visit. This does not mean rushing out and spending money redecorating your home. In fact, it is better for a man to see the way you live your everyday life.

Make sure your place is neat and tidy

Because of your busy schedule, you may overlook certain things. But remember that a man will likely notice untidiness and carelessness quickly. A piece of clothing left lying around or a dirty computer screen can easily slip your attention but may give him the wrong impression. Let's face it, even though most people agree couples should share household chores, some men still judge women by their ability to be a good housewife.

If you have children

In the early stages is not the time for you to see if he would get along with your children. A brief introduction if it's convenient would be sufficient. After that, it's best for them to become scarce. If they need supervision, it may be wise to employ a sitter for the night. Although he may be comfortable with kids, it could prove overwhelming for him on a first visit.

Make it a memorable occasion for both

Find out his favorite music and have it playing in the background while you enjoy a drink or snack. Since you are confident that things between you will work out allow him to feel at home. Show him where the ice and the drinks are so he can serve himself if he wishes.

A word of caution here. It's likely he will feel free to drop in on you unannounced afterward. Don't allow him to take such liberties; it shows lack of consideration for you. If he should do so, don't let him in. Let him know you have visitors, and suggest the next time he calls beforehand.

Being a hostess who cooks

In our survey, several women said if they had to do it again, they would not start cooking for their man before they settled down with him. Their men grew to expect them to cook regularly and were disappointed when they didn't.

In any case, it is not wise for you to devote your energies to cooking and serving on his first visit to your home. The spotlight should be on you and not on a meal; there are plenty of restaurants for that. When you feel like rewarding him later on, you can give him a taste of your culinary skills. Let your cooking be a bonus and not part of your regular duties. Depending on how they were brought up, some men believe it's a woman's responsibility to cook and clean. Modern day men know that these duties are shared equally between both parties in a relationship.

Living together before marriage

This is a big one. Should you live together with your lover before you tie the knot? People often refer to the words of their mothers and grandmothers: "Why buy the cow when you can get the milk for free?" meaning that a man may never marry a woman if he is already enjoying all the benefits of a wife without a marriage commitment.

This comment presupposes that the man is the one who receives the lion's share of the benefits in a marital union. But today, the above statement applies to women also because marriage should be considered an equal partnership. Hence the question is: Should two people in love agree to share themselves by living together before making a public commitment?

In my opinion, if the people involved have followed all the steps previously outlined then, "Yes," provided the decision is mutual and for the right reasons. The desire to spend more time together to get away from parents, or to save money are not sufficiently sound reasons for moving in with a mate.

Think about all the marriages that have ended, in many cases, after years of living hell, then ask yourself, How many of these marriages would have collapsed after a few months had the partners tried being together 24 hours a day instead of only on some nights and weekends?

Benefits of living together before marriage

I suggest using this time to discover more about the personal habits of your mate.

No matter how much you think you know about a person, you will uncover new things when you live together day in day out under the same roof. You will be exposed to habits, traits, and practices of your partner that you could not know unless you live together. You've likely heard stories of people who got married and, once they moved in together, discovered things about their mate they couldn't live with.

By living together, you will come face to face with his/her reaction under stress, boredom, fatigue, frustration, sickness, and money problems. Not that you can change these reactions, but being aware of them eliminates the surprise of finding out about difficulties after marriage. Sometimes the shock of discovering certain intimate details of your mate after wedlock can influence your behavior in the marriage. When you are confronted with the many difficult issues, you may say to yourself, "I never dreamed that he/she was like this." Sometimes this causes you to change your attitude toward your mate and the relationship.

When you live together, you should be able to answer these questions:

1. Does he/she get depressed when it's time to pay bills?

2. Does he/she get violent when angry?

3. Does he/she spend most of his/her spare time on the phone talking with friends?

4. Does he leave the toilet seat up?

5. Is he/she an excessive user of alcohol or drugs?

6. Is he/she a night person?

7. Is he/she as emotional with you as before? Is he/she still playful or suddenly become serious and businesslike with you?

8. Do you detect a selfish streak in his/her actions? Does he/she think we as opposed to I when dealing with everyday matters?

When you know the answers to these and similar questions, you can openly discuss them with your mate, then come up with compromises and adjustments to suit you both.

Discover if you and your partner are compatible

George, a businessman, and Tami, a store window decorator, had been dating for a while. Tami found George dashing, debonair, romantic, and full of energy. She is 35 and he is 55. But he seemed to like the hectic life of social activity, which Tami also enjoyed. They fell in love and decided to tie the knot. After about a year of marriage, Tami found that he was not as willing to participate in social activities as before. Instead, he preferred the quiet life at home when he was not spending extra hours at work.

Tami was surprised at the change of his attitude and wondered if she had done something to bring about this change. Now, although other aspects of the relationship are functioning fine, to Tami George does not seem as attractive and exciting as he used to. He seemed to have grown older in a short amount of time.

"Life has become unfulfilling for me. A part of me is slipping away as the days go by. I tried maintaining a social life without Jack, but it's just not the same. What can I do?"

This commonly occurs when there are significant age differences in a marriage. George found the energy to keep up with social activities while dating because he was motivated by the idea of winning Tami in a whirlwind courtship. It may be that George was never a social animal but this question never came up while they were dating because it seemed unnecessary. If George and Tami had decided to live together before getting married, it's likely they would have made this discovery before.

When a man is a loving and romantic partner, you assume he will be a good husband. It's only after you get married you may realize that you share little in common. Likewise, a woman may be a terrific social companion, but lacks what it takes to be a live-in wife. Living together requires sharing control and responsibilities. It is easy to talk about these matters, but you may not be able to prove how willing or capable your partner can be until you come face to face with problems that need resolving.

A case against living together before marriage

Many psychoanalysts and marriage counselors have openly spoken out against cohabitation before wedlock. Even though it sounds like common sense that a couple can learn the true extent of their compatibility by living together before marriage, statistics do not bear this out.

One such study, *Cohabitation and Divorce in Canada,* states:[39]

"The popular belief that cohabitation is an effective strategy in a high-divorce society rests on the common-sense notion that getting to know one another before marrying should improve the quality and stability of marriage. However, in this instance, it is looking more and more as if common sense is a poor guide."

This study shows that even when you take into account other factors (including those that led to cohabitation such as religion, parental divorce, age at marriage, etc.) and living together by itself accounted for a higher divorce rate.

Another study done by DeMaris and MacDonald, reports similar findings: [40]

"Despite a widespread public faith in premarital cohabitation as a testing ground for marital incompatibility, research to date indicates that cohabiters' marriages are less satisfactory and more unstable than those of non-cohabiters."

The conclusion is that, although researchers are unable to put their fingers on specific elements, they believe something about living together before marriage causes marital problems later.

Four factors to consider

If you do decide to move in with your partner without a formal commitment, keep these factors in mind:

1. Do not live with someone unless you know him/her for a while and you feel it is right to do so. It must also be clear in your mind the reasons for your joint decision to live together.

2. Set a time limit. If living together is a prerequisite to marriage, discuss this with your mate before you move in. Numerous surveys have shown that most women said their reason for living together was a step toward marriage. However, most men gave

readily available sex as their primary reason for cohabitation. You should also set an approximate time limit for living together. Studies show that a relationship will peak and then plateau (i.e., it reaches a peak and then levels off). That means you can reach a stage in your relationship where you lose the urge and excitement that once existed. If this happens before marriage, then the impetus for marriage could be lost.

3. Some psychologists claim that marriage does something to people that alters their mental state in a positive way. If the same peak and plateau syndrome mentioned above occurs in a state of matrimony, a couple is likely to seek solutions to save the marriage. However, in the absence of a formal commitment, the parties feel free to go their separate ways.

4. Live your life as you normally would. You may try to avoid conflict with your mate to maintain tranquility in the relationship. But remember that you want your mate to know your true character. Don't hesitate to express your dissatisfaction if something doesn't please you. It is better to let your partner know how you feel now than to withhold your feelings until after you're married.

A final word

Some people - be it for religious, moral, or other reasons - are against cohabitation before marriage. If your partner is one of these people, don't push it. A man may think less of a woman who is willing to live with a man, or a woman may see it as a sign of disrespect if a man asks her to move in with him.

I suggest you try to determine your partner's true motivation for not moving in with you. It could be that he/she is afraid you might discover things about his/her personality, which he/she would prefer you find out after you're married. You may be surprised to know how many people say, "So what if he/she finds out afterwards? By then, we would have already been to the altar."

If you truly want to learn more about your partner but living together is not an option, arrange to spend one or more weeks of total immersion together: Plan a skiing, camping, or fishing trip, or a vacation outside the country. Although one or two weeks together is not a good substitute, you will still be able to get an idea of how you get along as a couple.

If you believe the importance of knowing as much as you can about the person you plan to marry is being exaggerated here, think about the people who wake up and discover they are married to closet homosexuals, drug addicts, child molesters, chronic wife-beaters, sexaholics, and the lists goes on.

Many people are in denial about their problems. Sometimes they believe that finding a love partner can cure them. They may be clearly oblivious to the fact that relationships are not centers for professional treatment.

Chapter Nine
Making a commitment to each other

You have known each other for some time now. You feel that a reasonable level of compatibility exist between you. Your partner has demonstrated the desire, capability, and readiness to enter into a serious relationship with you. And you both feel in love with each other. Congratulations! You are ready to commit to a loving relationship.

You may decide on a legal wedding ceremony or, for the less traditional, a non-legal or private way of formalizing your commitment to each other. Whatever form you select, it is important to understand the true meaning of such commitment.

Your commitment to your mate is not your marriage license, your wedding ceremony, nor your living arrangements. When you commit, you are in fact agreeing to the following:

"After serious consideration and with full responsibility and integrity, I am agreeing to share my life with my partner; to assist in his/her personal growth development and happiness wherever and whenever I can. I also agree to cherish and protect this union with my partner so it can forever flourish and always remains a happy one. I am agreeing to this because I want to, and for no other reason."

When you look at marriage in this way, it becomes easier to see why a marriage commitment does not end with a ceremony. Instead, it becomes a commitment for two people to strive toward, on a day-to-day basis. The commitment is to ensure the continued growth of each other and the relationship.

I always remember the expression on a young lady's face when, one morning, she burst into the office where I worked. With excitement, pride, and contentment in her voice, she showed off her engagement ring. She had finally received a marriage proposal from a young man whom we all considered to be one of the most eligible bachelors around. She was the envy of all the women.

I later learned she had confided in close friends that, although she had hoped for a marriage proposal, she had not really expected one. She confessed that she had done all she could to win her fiancé, and that she was glad that it was over now. No, it is not over yet. Too many people see marriage as a point of arrival instead of the beginning of a long journey.

Too many people support the belief that after they have taken the necessary steps to secure a marriage commitment, they can relax in the comfort that their work is done. This kind of thinking can cause complacency, which is one of the killers of love relationships. I am reminded of an old saying: "The same things you did to win your partner are the same things you should do to keep him/her."

Yes, there are good reasons to celebrate when two people decide to commit to each other in a loving relationship, but remember that this is only the beginning. Celebrate that you have been blessed with the good fortune to find a mate who has met your standards for eligibility, and that you have both fallen in love with each other.

You must also realize that an offer of a commitment is a demonstration of the highest regard and a great compliment of love. When your partner offers marriage or another form of formal commitment to you for the right reasons, he/she is saying you have been placed as the highest priority in his/her life. Treasure this commitment and use your relationship as a launching ground. This launching ground marks the beginning of a new journey, which can take you to new places in life you've only dreamed about.

Your relationship responsibilities

In the context of a loving relationship, responsibility does not only mean tasks, obligations, etc. Yes, always assist your partner with household chores, financial support, marital duties, etc. But responsibility in a relationship has a much broader definition. Romantic relationships provide an environment in which to learn who you really are in relation to the person you're with. This is not to say you need someone else to discover your true self. But being with a partner helps in sharing love, something you cannot do alone. To truly enjoy love, you have to express it with others.

Many people believe they are on this earth for a purpose, that their existence will benefit mankind. Perhaps their contribution may not be as important as that of Alexander Graham Bell or Mother Theresa, but in some way will have a positive impact on society. A comedian, who makes people laugh or a mother whose daughter may discover a cure for the HIV virus are both important to our society.

Most people spend years trying to find a purpose for their existence. Some are lucky to discover what they believe to be their purpose relatively early in life. Others do so much later. And many people go through their entire lives without finding what they believe to be the true purpose for their existence.

When that discovery happens, you experience a marked change in life, which produces a profound impact on your existence. A person who has been converted to a religious calling or who decided to devote his/her life to a special cause falls into this category. Every day is full of excitement and a desire to constantly move forward. Fulfillment from the cause provides new energy.

Most people strive to arrive at this point in life. Within a loving relationship, it's your partner's responsibility to help bring out the hidden qualities you may not know you possessed. This does not mean you should sit by waiting for your partner to guide you toward your goals and dreams. It means that because of the love and mutual caring that exists between you, your partner will be aware of your emotional and spiritual struggles and provide encouragement and assistance with these struggles.

I've heard many happy couples say their partner represents their "other half." Now that they have found each other, they feel complete. This is one of the many myths surrounding romantic love. You may need others to assist in the development of certain areas, but no one can complete you, because you are already complete. If you can be happy by yourself, only then can you find happiness with someone else.

The secret is to feel comfortable defining yourself without having to include another person. For example, Mr. Smith's daughter or Mr. Jones's wife. When you depend on others to make you complete, you assume a position of inferiority. And it's for this reason some people feel lost and incomplete after a breakup in their relationship.

Remember if you seek happiness from outside, you will always be disappointed. True happiness comes from within. Yes, you can benefit from what your partner brings to the relationship, but you should not lose any part of you if what he/she brings is ever taken away.

The desire to nurture the one you love comes automatically when you are in love. Of course this refers to a mature love relationship. This is a relationship in which both parties are concerned with the needs of each other, not when one or both are interested only in their own needs.

People who love their significant other do not need to be told when she/he needs to be comforted, when he/she needs to be held, stroked and caressed, and when he/she needs to be left alone with his/her own thoughts.

You believe that your partner can succeed in whatever he/she sets out to accomplish and you respect his/her opinions no matter how childish or insignificant they may seem. Some people, even though they are in love with their mates, have not learned the art of (or feel the need for) nurturing. This can have roots in their upbringing, but it is easy to see why they would feel loved and appreciated when their partner nurtures them.

Why people marry

According to Burnham and Phelan in their very informative book "*Mean Genes*" [41] humans are guided by their genes whose primary purpose is to ensure the continuation of the species. Both men and women pursue their genetic goals in whatever way seems most efficient. Marriage is one of these ways. It is an exchange between two people. The man offers commitment, protection, and financial support while the woman contributes the promise of sexual exclusivity, caring, and fertility. Traditionally, a man is expected to give her a ring as proof of his ability to provide material goods, and the woman's virginity proves she has kept herself pure and is now ready to be the exclusive property of her husband to be.

From as far back as we know, marriage has been the accepted structure of a family unit: When you're ready to start a family you get married.

Traditionally, families took a special interest in the selection of a marriage partner for their offspring to preserve the customs and traditions of their clans and communities. In the custom of arranged marriages, two people were brought together by community elders and matchmakers, and marriages took the form of a business arrangement between two families. It was even customary in some cases for the bride's family to offer a dowry, i.e., a gift of money or property in order to sweeten the deal. The wishes of the marriage couple in such an arrangement were of little importance. Of importance was having as many children as they were able to, and carrying on the family's tradition.

Except for a few cases, arranged marriages are no longer practiced in the United States, but are still common in certain societies. And with the problem of overpopulation in the world today, people ask, "Why should I get married, especially when I can support myself, and I don't want to have children?"

Some people mistakenly believe that marriage originated from a legal or religious obligation. This is not the case. In every society, marriage has always been a choice between two people and only sanctioned by the Church and State. Clearly, marriage is a choice and not an obligation. When two people choose to marry, it is then and only then do the Church and State intervene to provide legal protection for the marriage. [42]

However, recent actions on the part of government and state indicate these practices might be changing. In February, 2002, Frank Keating, governor of the state of Oklahoma, allocated 10 million of federal tax dollars to a program intended to combat divorce and promote heterosexual marriage in the state. In officially proclaiming February 13 as "Sanctity of Marriage Day," the governor urged churches and religious groups statewide to develop special programs aimed at improving marriages.

Surely we can understand the practical consideration of marriage: the protection of children, questions of family inheritance, etc., but there is nothing wrong with people who choose to live together without the formal commitment of marriage. In fact, in most modern societies today, there are similar laws to protect people who live together without a marriage contract.

Are people still committed to marriages?

The concept of marriage has always been, "Until death do us part." Today, to many people, it's more like "As long as I'm happy." And nowadays, even the interpretation of this happiness can vary.

For various reasons, we sometimes find it difficult to communicate our personal needs and expectations to our partners. Such needs and expectations can change from time to time due to changing circumstances in our lives. For example, you and your partner might have come together because of your mutual desire to travel and explore the universe. But your life's direction may change after you've had your fill of adventure from traveling.

Also, sometimes we ourselves do not fully understand the implications of what we ask or expect from our partnership. And since misunderstandings can be the order of the day in many love relationships, we ought to maintain constant communication, both verbal and non-verbal, clearly expressing what we expect from our mates. Maintaining the flexibility to regroup and renegotiate our understanding of our relationship agreement from time to time also helps.

For a long time, it was customary to honor your commitment in marriage. Once you made it, you lived by it. But many people who, after 25 or more years of unhappy marriages, confessed that they remained together only because of their commitment. Of course our society assisted in the prolongation of unhappy marriages by making it difficult to get a divorce.

A change of the laws in the United States made divorces easier and brought many people in unhappy marriages out of the closet. Now it is common to get a divorce when it becomes clear your marriage has ceased to function. Some marriage counselors do not support the concept of easy divorce. They believe marriage works best when there is a strong commitment between two people. They say that making it difficult to obtain a divorce forces people to honor their commitment to each other.

Remember the saying "You can lead a horse to water, but you can't make him drink." Similarly, you can convince someone you are their best choice for marriage, but you cannot force him/her to love you if you subsequently become unlovable. It is my belief that commitment does not make a happy marriage but, when the marriage is a happy one, the partners become emotionally and morally committed to each other.

PART 2

Sharing Your Lives Together

Chapter Ten

What do men and women want from a relationship?

Couples in love, despite their good intentions and desire to maintain a happy relationship together, often encounter unexpected problems, which cause tension and unhappiness in their lives.

Here's what usually happens when the pressures of everyday life begin to take its toll. You begin to have disagreements; small issues become big ones; normal discussions develop into heated arguments, which escalate into fights and quarrels.

Then comes the breakdown in communications when each partner withdraws to himself or herself. Before you know it, they talk about separation. Harvard psychiatrists Richard Schwartz and Jacqueline Olds observe that most long term relationships go through a natural pattern of ebb and flow; sometimes there are high points and sometimes there is a decline. In their book *Marriage in Motion,* they noted that most people are not aware of this natural process that is common in long term relationships. So when people experience a low point in the relationship, they automatically assume that the decline is a downhill trend to disaster. [43]

And because people get bogged down with the complexities

of everyday living and stress, they devote little energy in trying to repair the damage. The result is that well-intentioned people arrive at a point of hopelessness and bewilderment, wondering how they got there.

Now that you are sharing your life with a love partner, it is important to understand some of the primary reasons why relationships fail. Men and women approach the subject of relationships differently. And even though they both have the same goals, their different approaches can result in misunderstandings between them, which can further complicate matters. To be successful in a relationship, both men and women must understand what their prospective mate wants from the relationship. Sometimes it is difficult to fully understand a partner's motivations for entering the relationship.

What do women want?

Over the years, I have been involved in countless discussions, hundreds of one-on-one conversations, and dozens of in-depth interviews on this subject. My personal experiences plus the information I obtained from several psychological studies and opinions have led me to the following conclusions:

1. The principal reason relationships fail is because there is a great misunderstanding between men and women. Each party seems to be confused about what the other seeks in a relationship.

2. Both men and women want basically the same things from a relationship. To love and to be loved, to be cherished, to have great sex and intimacy, to be number one, to be respected, trusted, and so on. I have collected hundreds of answers.

3. Men and women have different ways of achieving what they want from each other. Yet this misunderstanding that exists between the sexes has been a stumbling block to creating great

relationships, even before the relationship begins. But sadly enough, what men think that women want from them and what women believe that men want is not generally true for the majority of men and women.

For example, instead of entering relationships feeling valued for who they are as human-beings, most people enter a relationship expecting to be used for what they can bring to the relationship. Why? Because men believe women primarily want them for financial and other security reasons, and women think men primarily want them for sex and to take care of their dirty laundry.

So both men and women begin a relationship with resentment and a feeling of competitiveness: "I am going to deliver what he/she wants, but only if he/she gives me what I want." Herein lies the root-cause of the problems between the sexes.

If somehow men could learn what women really want and women could understand what men really want, we may someday see a marked improvement in how the sexes relate with each other.

What men need to understand about women

Let's examine an age-old saying: "Women themselves don't know what they really want." I believe such statements originated with and are commonly held by men, only because most men do not understand women.

My belief is that most women have good ideas of what they want from a relationship and become discontented when they believe they are not getting enough. Like all human-beings, a woman's wants can change from time to time. Every woman is different; they don't like to be classified. However, to achieve what they want depends on their man's understanding of women. Misunderstandings between men and women existed from as far back as most of us care to remember. But it has come more to the forefront today because society has changed so much.

For centuries women have been accommodating to men, perhaps as a means of ensuring their survival. It was the man's responsibility to provide food, and shelter, and in perilous times, protection for his family. Today, some men instinctively expect women to be as accommodating as they were in the past. But times have changed and providing for a family is no longer a life-threatening task for a man (except if he is a drug dealer). And in many cases, women can and do provide for their families just as efficiently as men.

Now, modern women do not see the need to be as accommodating to their men as their great grandmothers were simply because they are good providers. Today's women need more; they need emotional support from men. A great many women do not know how to effectively communicate their emotional needs to their men. So they try to please men in the traditional fashion in the hope that, in return, they give them the emotional support they need.

But some men just don't get it. And when the woman continues to make the effort to please men in the traditional fashion, they usually work themselves into a state of exhaustion. Cooking, cleaning, child rearing, being a hostess and a sex partner can become tiring to women who feel they are not receiving their men's support. The result is deep resentment for the men they hold responsible for their situation.

Even though a woman may still love her husband, she finds it difficult to show love under these circumstances. She may become unhappy. When some men see their women unhappy, they mistakenly assume their unhappiness indicates that they (the men) have failed as providers. A man's solution is to work harder in an effort to provide more for his family. Of course, working harder means devoting more time to work projects while leaving less time to devote to his relationship.

Instead of improving, the situation gets worse. The man burns himself out trying to please the woman the only way he knows how. Frustration may step in, and the man may withdraw within himself, believing that no matter what he does, his woman is not happy. "What can I do to please her? What does a woman want?"

- **A woman wants confidence.**

Women are immediately attracted to men who demonstrate personal confidence. A woman longs to have at her side a man who, by his actions, says, "You don't have to worry; whatever comes up I can handle it." I'm not referring to arrogance, useless bravado, or superman status. I refer to a man who is so secure in himself that he is not afraid to take on responsibilities - the kind of man who says, "I can handle it... somehow."

A woman likes to know her man will take control of a situation and see it through to completion. He is not ashamed to seek advice and willingly take responsibility if things go wrong.

- **A woman needs a man who can bring out the best in her.**

I once interviewed a woman who has been married to the same man for 18 years. I selected her because I knew she and her husband enjoyed an excellent romantic love relationship with each other. She was 48. I asked her to tell me her secret to a successful marriage.

"From the first time I met my husband, I knew he was the man for me. It was a small but noisy restaurant on the East Side in New York. We spent hours talking, or should I say I talked and he listened. He wanted to know about my dreams, desires, and feelings. He asked questions and listened carefully to my answers. For some reason, I felt at ease to freely express emotions that I had never expressed to anyone else; he had found a way to draw them out of me. I felt that he had great interest in me, and I was right.

"As I got to know him better, he searched for and found qualities in me that even I did not know I possessed. He encouraged and developed me. I am what I am today because of him. (She is a successful corporate manager of a retail chain and a mother of two wonderful children.) But there is more.

"He surrendered completely to me; he gave me power over his heart and soul. I felt as if he belonged to me. At no time in our relationship did I feel jealous or insecure of him. I trusted him completely. Even after all these years, there is nothing that I wouldn't do for him, not because he asks but because I always want to."

Women may not consciously articulate this, but these are the qualities many women seek in a man - a man who can identify and draw out her special talents and abilities. Every woman has special talents waiting to be developed. However, it takes a special man who cares enough for her to bring these qualities to the surface.

A great many women are on the lookout for such a man and when they find him, they fall in love. A woman needs a man who believes so much in her that he is not afraid to entrust her with his most intimate feelings. She needs a man who puts himself completely in his woman's hands.

When a man empowers a woman over him by completely surrendering to her, the woman feels so loved and cherished that she cannot help but return the same trust, love, and support to the man. This uninhibited sharing of love empowers both of them simultaneously. And this, folks, is the kind of union that forms the solid foundation necessary for a successful and lasting love relationship.

Unfortunately, many men are not aware of this primary need that women possess. Instead, they think women need them for financial security and other such reasons. And for this and other reasons, men are reluctant to expose their innermost feelings to their women. Some men fear their women may see this as a sign of vulnerability and seize the opportunity to control them. Of course, this is a man's way: planning and devising strategies to achieve his goal.

But do women really want to control men? In some cases probably, but for the majority of women, this is not true. Women need men who will share intimacy with them. According to Dr. Nathaniel Branden, true intimacy can only be shared between equals. [44]

- **She needs a man who can fill different roles.**

For generations, society has given men permission to have another woman while still being married to their wives. Men have always believed that since one woman cannot satisfy their every need, they are entitled to seek others if they so desire. Even today, this way of thinking has not changed much. I asked a seven-year old boy what he would like to be when he grows up. He replied, "I want to be rich so I can have lots of women." Indeed, we have seen that Americans were not upset with President Bill Clinton because he had a mistress, but because he lied about it.

During the time of the Bill Clinton affair, the Russian people were asked in an opinion poll what would be their reaction if their president was exposed in a similar scandal. The majority of Russians surveyed said they would be glad because it would show that their president is human.

Society, however, does not afford the same luxury of "humanness" to women. A woman is supposed to find her knight in shining armor and put up with whatever shortcomings he may have. Even in today's world, having more than one man at the same time is just not acceptable if you are a woman.

Today's woman may choose to live by society's impositions, but demands that her Mr. Right at least be capable of meeting all her needs. In all fairness to women, this is not too much to ask, is it? Nowadays, it is no longer sufficient for a man to be just a good provider. Women are seeking men who can be versatile in their roles as husbands. In addition to being her hero (i.e., a guy who will sweep her off her feet and protect her from life's economic and other problems), he must also be her soul mate, her romantic lover, and her playmate.

But here's the problem. Most men are not built that way. Psychologists have observed that men, by their nature, focus on only one goal at a time. When that goal is achieved, they then switch their focus to other objectives. And according to marital therapists, this explains why men seem to be less romantic after they get married. [45]

Consider this. When a man is in hot pursuit of a woman he cares about, he stops at nothing in his effort to win her. He stays awake until the wee hours of the morning in conversations with her, ignoring that he has to work the next day. He goes out of his way to be romantic even though he may not be the romantic type. I myself have traveled hundreds of miles just to spend two hours with a woman I was crazy about. No doubt a woman will be moved by the man's intense desire to prove his love for her. She may see nothing but good times ahead.

You can imagine her surprise after she enters a relationship with him and he ceases to be as romantic as he was. A woman who is not familiar with men's behavior patterns would conclude he has stopped loving her. On the contrary, he may love her even more, now that they have become intimate partners. However, the way he demonstrates his love for her may change. The man may rationalize that, now that he has taken on new responsibilities, his main goal is to be a good provider. He redirects his energies with renewed vigor to earning money. Unfortunately, many men do not realize how important it is to continue the romance after the initial courtship.

They mistakenly believe women would see the extra sacrifice they make as an indication of their increased love. But instead, the woman feels that when a man focuses on his job more than on the relationship, it means he has stopped caring for her.

She feels ignored because it seems like his job has become more important than her. Gerry, 37, an insurance salesman says, "I just don't know what else to do. At first she was upset that there was never enough money to buy her the things she liked. I solved that problem by busting my chops to earn more. Now she nags me about not spending enough time with her. You can't win, can you?"

What can men do?

A man has to find ways to balance work and home activities. This is easier said than done. Remember that no matter what people say, it is hard to erase from men's minds the belief that women primarily need them for material success in the outer world. This is the only way a man can feel safe; he will always believe the rug will not be pulled from under him if he is financially successful.

Even when he tries to convince himself there is more to life than money, he is bombarded daily by media messages. "Give her a diamond and she'll love you forever" or "Drive a BMW; people will know you've made it." So a man takes no chances.

"Show me the money; I'll work on the relationship later." But men have to face the fact that the relationship is just as important as their work. They are wise to make a conscious effort to pay more attention to their women.

Treat your relationship as part of your job

A marriage counselor suggested to my friend Robert that he pretends his relationship is part of his work. Robert was so programmed to focus on his work that he could not convince himself to devote time to his family. By the time he arrived home at the end of the day, he was too tired to do anything but to sit in front of the TV and fall asleep. It was only when his wife finally separated from him for a while and took the kids with her that he decided to do something.

The marriage counselor observed that one reason Robert was so successful was that he was disciplined to focus on the task at hand until it was completed. So he suggested Robert include one hour a day in his regular schedule and call it family hour. This means if he works for eight hours at the office, he should schedule nine hours for his day's work. When he does arrive home, he must devote one hour to doing things with his wife and children. He doesn't even need to tell his wife what he is doing. All he has to do is to offer to help her with chores, listen to her when she tells him how her day went, and so on. But he must remember to treat this hour as a continuation of his job. Only after the hour has passed, can he say he has concluded his day's work.

It would probably be difficult for a boxer who has just been declared the winner of a 14-round fight to go another two rounds. This is because he paced himself to complete 14 rounds and gave it all he had. If asked to go another round, he would have to reprogram his system to focus on a new task, which would be difficult. Similarly, a man experiences a feeling of accomplishment when he has completed a day's work, more so if he feels his day has been successful. He then feels justified in rewarding himself with some well-earned rest, maybe a strong drink and a read of the newspaper. His most important task is completed. He is pleased to have produced one more day of income that would provide the things needed to make the woman he loves happy and contented. He may even pat himself on the back.

Like most men, my friend Robert was not aware of the importance that emotional support plays in a woman's life. It took the shock of his wife's leaving him to realize what was at stake. Sometimes people need drastic actions to bring them face to face with the problem at hand. Her departure made him see the importance of giving his woman what she needed most.

After sometime, Robert moved back in with his family and within 12 months, their relationship has shown great signs of improvement.

- **A woman wants to be a woman.**

Men today complain they are not getting from their women what they once got in the past. Cooking, cleaning, and caretaking are just not the high points in women's life nowadays as it was in the days of their grandmothers. This coincides with a joke I recently heard on CHFI, a Toronto radio station.

While walking in the woods, a modern-day princess encountered a frog. As she observed the lonely creature, to her surprise it began to speak. "Oh! My princess, have pity on me. I am a victim of a great injustice." In tears, the frog began to explain. "You see, I was a handsome prince who has fallen prey to a wicked witch. She cast a spell on me and turned me into the sorry state I am in today. But you, my Princess, if you wish, can save me from my misfortune. All you have to do is to kiss me and I will be restored to my original self. I will once again be a handsome prince. In return for your good deed, I will take you to my palace where you will become my wife. There you can cook, clean, take care of my palace, and be happy and eternally grateful to me."

That night, the princess sat in her dining room enjoying her tasty dinner of frog's legs: She reflected on her day's events and thought, "No, I don't think so."

But the desire to nurture still is and will always be an integral part of a woman's make up. However, modern-day men are wise to understand that a woman's need to nurture is not a desire to become a servant, and that the support of a good woman can greatly enhance a man's strength. Numerous studies show that a man who is happy in his home life is more likely to be successful at his work. [46] In preparing his world-famous best-seller *Think and Grow Rich*, Napoleon Hill interviewed 500 of the most successful men in America. He wanted to know some of their secrets to success. Surprisingly, all these men were happily married to the same woman, and had been so for over 30 years. Hill was convinced that, "behind every successful man there is a great woman."

Throughout history, women were not expected to be the providers for their families; that has always been a man's job. But today's economic realities have forced women to take on the additional role as provider or co-provider. Many men say they just couldn't make it without the additional support of the wife's income.

This change puts women in direct conflict with their femininity. Traditionally being feminine meant, among other things, depending on a man's support as a provider. And even though today's women do not depend on men this way, some still believe providing for his family is principally a man's responsibility, according to our survey. Some women feel the moment they no longer need a man's financial support, they are giving more than he is to the relationship. She also feels less feminine because she has taken on the man's role. And although she may not immediately understand why, she may become less and less turned on by him. [47] This is even worse if she had not been receiving emotional support from the man all along.

This has evolved not because women do not like to work outside of the home. In fact, many women enjoy having a career and the independence that goes with it. Also, a woman who loves her husband would do whatever it takes to assist him, and many women work even though they may not want to do so.

However, women become resentful when they believe the man does not appreciate their sacrifice. In effect, these women are saying, "I have given up part of who I am out of the necessity to maintain the environment where I can continue to share love with you. The least you can do is to return the love by giving me the emotional support to replenish the part of me that I sacrificed."

But most women don't usually voice their resentment to their partners. Some of them may not even be consciously aware of what's taking place. All they know is that something is missing but they cannot put their finger on the problem. So they become focused on fulfilling their new responsibilities while maintaining their traditional roles as nurturers to their partners. They may reason, "My family needs me. I must do my best not to let them down." Some men may have experienced their women being overly concerned with being efficient and completing tasks. Instead of relaxing when she gets home from work, she aggressively moves on to doing housework, tidying up the house, watering the plants, preparing lunches for the next day. She doesn't stop until all tasks are completed.

Here's where the man can make a difference.

It is of vital importance for a man to understand what's happening when a woman is in an auto drive-mode. This is the time when he is most needed.

Many men assume a woman in this state needs to be left alone. This is a mistake because here lies a major difference between women's and men's behavior. When a man comes home stressed, he usually wants to retreat to where he can be by himself. He finds himself in front of the TV or reads a magazine. He may become irritable if his wife tries to initiate a conversation. A woman is exactly the opposite. When she feels stressed, she experiences relief by talking, says John Gray Ph.D.,[48]

How a man can nurture a woman's female side.

John Gray, Ph.D., observes that a woman who has experienced stress in a goal-related work environment finds relief if she can come home to a loving and caring relationship. At work, most of her conversations are focused on solving problems, getting to the bottom line. By the time she gets home, she does not want to hear another customer complaint or know about the new system of recruiting competent staff. She wants to talk about people, feelings, her children, her friends, birthdays, weddings, and such things. Her conversations are not channeled in the direction of finding solutions to problems; she just wants a personal discussion. [49]

If her partner pays attention to what she says and does not necessarily suggests remedies or solutions, a woman can find relief from the stress caused because she is being forced to play a man's role. Gradually, she feels more like a woman because she can spontaneously and emotionally express herself.

Guys, be careful not to make this mistake.

Many well-intentioned men, who are not familiar with this aspect of women's behavior, try to persuade their wives not to take on too much. It may be true that women get carried away maintaining ancient family traditions, thus placing unreasonable burdens on themselves. For example, my wife still insists on making an apple pie from scratch. And of course I love to eat fresh apple pie. However, it may be unrealistic and unnecessary for a woman to do all the things she would like to. And although men may want to show their support in these circumstances, they have to be careful how they communicate their intentions.

For example, a man might say to his partner, "You're taking on too much." But she may mistakenly take it to mean (a) that he doesn't appreciate or value what I am doing for him, or (b) if you spend all evening working, what time would you have for me? or (c) if he thinks what I am doing is not important, then he would never give me the emotional support I need.

Guys, here's some advice. Never say to a woman, "If you are going to do it and complain, just don't do it." Or "You think this is hard, you should see what I have to do at the plant."

- **A woman wants a man to always be masculine.**

Indeed the good man may not be hard to find,
but the question is;
would you want him after you found him?
—Regina Barreca

Women often say they would like to be with a sensitive man, a man who is in touch with his feelings and is not afraid to express them. Yet I know of numerous women who are still dissatisfied after they find such a man. Why?

The bottom line is that a woman needs a man who is in close touch with his masculinity. It's true that she may need a man who is not afraid to express his feelings sometimes. But what she also needs is a man who is strong but is sensitive to her needs. A man has to know how far to go when opening up to a woman. If a man constantly pours out his heart to his woman, she may feel burdened and even insecure. If he persists, she may even become annoyed. Remember, no matter how strong and self-sufficient a woman might appear, she still usually looks to her man for support. If it turns out the man feels needy for her support, she may lose her attraction for him as a man. She may still love him but some of the passion in the relationship may die.

Masculinity to a woman signifies the following:

1. Security. Today's women are independent and can take care of themselves; they don't need a man to protect them as they did in past generations. However, it seems like society still considers a man as a symbol of security for a woman. Maude, a single mom, said she keeps a pair of men's shoes and coat in plain sight whenever a repairman or other stranger comes to visit her home. She does this to give the stranger the impression a man lives there. This way, a tradesman is more likely to do a fair job.

To today's woman, security likely means a safe and comfortable environment where she can freely express her emotions. A relationship with a strong man who is himself secure provides such an environment. When a man cares for a woman and listens to her without getting annoyed or impatient, he becomes very valuable to the woman.

2. Strength. This means not necessarily physical but emotional, inner strength. Women want a man who knows what he wants and is prepared to do what it takes to get it: A man who has the strength to say yes or no and live by his decision; a man who can satisfy his partners needs and the needs of the relationship without sacrificing himself in the process.

Understanding men

For years, women have been trying without success to get their men to be closer to the kind of men they want. Some just don't know what more to do, while others have totally given up. And because many women do not understand the complex nature of men's behavior, they blame them for the dilemma in which they find themselves today.

But are men really to blame? Let's look at things from the man's side. A man may love his woman and sincerely want to express his love to her, but his life-long training and conditioning prevents him from doing so in the way that a woman expects. From childhood, a boy was taught to be alone, to hide his emotions, not to feel pain, to be calm at all times, and not to show fear. "Never lose your head over a girl," he was told.

Several years ago, my friend Lance and I drove down a busy street in a small town. I was thinking what a hot day it was when Lance got my attention. "Look," he said pointing to two gorgeous, well-dressed women who were about to cross the street. He tapped me on the shoulder as I turned my head to look. "Don't look directly, but aren't they beautiful?" Afterward I told him I did find the women attractive and asked him what was wrong in looking directly at them. He explained that a man should never let a woman know how great an impression she makes on him. "Why?" I asked. "Because afterward she plays hard to get," he replied.

So, like good students, men learned well. And now that they have graduated to become the men they've been taught to be, their women blame them for being who they are. No wonder men are so confused.

But a man can be an important compliment to a woman, so it's in women's interest to teach men what women already know about the inner world. To do this, women need to have a better understanding of men.

Men need women more than they know or will admit

Men may complain about how difficult it is to live with women, but the fact is that men need women. Just look at the statistics. According to Masters & Johnson, 94% of all men marry. And divorced men remarry more quickly than divorced women. [50]

Women also compliment men's lives, for obvious reasons like companionship and reproduction, but a greater need is the link women provide to reconnect men with the inner world. This is the world of feelings, love, intuition, and relationships. This is the world from which men became separated a long time ago. To a great extent women have succeeded, today's men are much more in touch with their inner feelings than their predecessors. However, the process has been slow and many men still don't feel comfortable openly expressing feelings. [51]

In addition to fulfilling their emotional needs, women also take care of men's physical needs, for example, they make sure that they eat well and see a doctor if they become ill. Men are not generally known for keeping close relationships with other men and women. However, most men do not rest until they find one woman with whom they can share love and intimacy; men are constantly on the lookout for a soul mate.

I strongly believe that, contrary to popular opinion, the majority of men do not need nor want to have more than one woman at the same time. I think this is a myth that has gained popularity because of the large numbers of men who seek other relationships when they cease to find fulfillment in their principal relationship. When a man finds a soul mate who loves and fulfills him, he forms a bond he expects to last a lifetime, "until death do us part."

Men experience a natural pull toward women, but sometimes even men themselves do not fully understand the power of this attraction. In her book Love in America, Francesca Cancian refers to a study that reported a 40% higher death rate among men whose wives had died within the past six months.

The study also said that divorced men commit suicide five times more than married men. [52]

Men always seem to need more sex than they get

A survey carried out by a popular magazine Psychology Today found that of the men surveyed, 55% were dissatisfied with their sex lives.

This seems to be a universal problem among men. Studies show that men think about sex six times an hour. And the average married couple has sex one to five times a week. Do you wonder why pornography is a multibillion dollar business? Men spend a lot of time fantasizing about sex and longing to have more. [53] This problem exists because men and women approach sex in different ways. Men show their affection by their sexual performance; women need affection to make them ready for sex. So a great many men and women go through life in a love-sex conflict; he complains that he is not getting enough sex from her and she longs for him to be more romantic with her. (The reasons for this difference in men and women's behavior are explained in Chapter 11 "Sex, are men getting enough?"

So men believe they're getting a raw deal. This is how a man sees it. He makes a lifelong commitment to remain faithful to his woman who to him, means she will be his only sexual partner. He believes this because, during courtship, he was led to believe she was just as interested in sex with him as he was with her. He assumed that at least they were sexually compatible. Now that they are married, she no longer seems interested in sex as she was before; it's as if she tricked him, he may rationalize. Of course this may not be true, but if not handled properly, this situation could be the beginning of a downhill trend in the relationship.

Men need to have their egos fed

On a CNN Network report, a man was being interviewed at the

scene of a fire where he risked his life to save a child who had been trapped in the burning building. The reporter commented, "That was a very heroic act you just performed. How do you feel?" The man replied, "It was nothing that great; I just did what any man would have done." [54]

Our society has always expected men to portray an image of competence, strength, courage, and independence. This is how a man is supposed to be; he does not need to be praised for who he is. And men try to live up to society's expectations by not seeking to claim special status for being just who they are.

The truth is, like most people, men do need to feel appreciated for who they are and what they do, even though they may not say so. Women have always openly expressed their need to be complimented, praised, and admired. However, if a man needed to have his ego stroked, she might think of him as weak or childish. And although today's woman is becoming more and more familiar with this aspect of men's behavior, many women still live by the old rules.

So a man has to be careful not to seem too needy for praise from his woman. Imagine how annoyed a woman may feel if her husband wants her to say nice things to him when she feels he is not saying nice things to her. So here again, men find themselves having to live up to what people expect them to be instead of being who they are.

Knowing this, a woman ought to make a special effort to tell her man how valuable he is to her. Every time he does something nice, she should tell him how much she appreciates the gesture. This will not only encourage him to do more nice things for her, but will also make him feel good about himself. The better a man feels about himself in her company, the more likely he is to remain in love.

Men still do not feel comfortable expressing emotions

For generations, men have always been reluctant to openly show emotions. However, we wanted to know how modern-day men felt about expressing their love to women. We interviewed men of various age groups and here are some of the comments we received.

"I would buy her gifts, bring her flowers, and even remember her birthday, but talk about love? Well. That's another story. You tell a woman you love her and she thinks she owns you. It's a trap," said Antonio, 48, a divorced chef at a Greek restaurant.

Mike, a 33-year-old pet store manager, said, "It's all about trust. To tell a woman I love her, I have to know her long enough to trust her. I know too many guys who fell in love too quickly but were disappointed later to find out that things were not what they seemed. Women want to hear the words "I love you" because then you're committed and it's hard to break off if you change your mind."

Men are scared of rejection, said Jules, "What happens if I tell her I love her and then I find out she doesn't love me. It's scary" Jules, a 24-year-old bank teller said a man must feel secure with the woman and know she feels the same way about him.

When a woman says "I love you," she does so spontaneously. When a man feels a strong emotional attraction to a woman, he becomes less articulate, and usually nervous. He may even fumble for words. The words "I love you" may come out but usually not from the deep feeling of attraction he may be experiencing. They come out because he believes it's the right thing to do when you experience such feelings.

Once he realizes a woman loves to hear these words, he

becomes more comfortable saying them. Again, not out of spontaneity, but as a means to an end: to please the woman. Realizing this, women should encourage men to express their feelings of love more often. According to John Gray, PhD., if he says it often enough, it may become a part of him and, who knows, one day men may even learn to express their feelings of love spontaneously.

But whether they express it or not, men do love women and different types of men love women differently. So a woman is wise to understand what special meaning love holds for the man she's with.

Men express their love in different ways

Some men feel like they've reached the end of their rope with women because women insist on judging men by their own standards for love. A man may not always want to hold hands while walking in the park, but he may cancel his long-planned fishing trip so that he can take his wife on vacation. "Sometimes I spend three weeks at a time sitting behind the wheel of my rig because I know she needs extra money for the household. Doesn't this mean that I love her?" asked Dave, a long-distance truck driver.

Another way some men express their love is by being controlling.

"When I first met Larry, I felt he was the man of my dreams" said Sharon, a 20-year-old graphics designer. "It seemed like we were spending every minute of our available time together. And when he was not with me, we talked for hours on the telephone. He called me every hour to find out where I was and what I was doing. At first, this seemed romantic; I believed he cared so much for me, he did not want to let me out of his sight not even for a minute.

"It has been a year and a half since we have been together and he still wants to know where I go and what I do when I am not with him. My friends say he is too controlling and maybe they're right, but I still believe he does so because he loves me."

To be controlling with someone is not necessarily a demonstration of love, however, some people accept it as a sign they are being cared for. And as Sharon explained, it does give her a sense of security. "Sure, it upsets me sometimes that he is so controlling, but I feel better this way. Anyway, I know I am always on his mind, which means I am also controlling him."

It's easier than you think.

You may be surprised to learn that your man is not as difficult to please as you thought. So make the effort to learn about the man with whom you choose to share your life. Find out what it takes to make him feel appreciated and try to do it.

Show him that even though you might not fully agree with all of his ways, you understand them. Meanwhile, praise him for the things he does right so he will be encouraged to do more. The misconception that women are determined to make them more like women has been a bugbear with men for centuries. However, when men learn what women really want, they are pleasantly surprised to discover what little it takes to make their women happy.

Just as for women, the way to a man's heart is through love. When a man knows the woman he is with truly loves him, he usually stays with her.

Chapter Eleven
Sex, are men getting enough?

Whether we admit it or not, our parents' sexual behavior has had a profound influence on our sex lives even in adulthood. Their actions, what they said and didn't say about sex, formed an important part in our interpretation of sexuality. Since our parents were probably conservative and hence discreet in their action, we may have been misled by some of their behavior. For example, you might have thought that your parents never slept together because they always had two separate beds in their bedroom. And since you have never heard them discussing sex, you might have assumed they never had sex.

This was exactly the case of a friend of mine until he was 17 years old and discovered by accident his parents often had sex. He was shocked; he couldn't believe they actually did it.

The misconceptions and false beliefs that men and women hold about sex are one of the major reasons relationships are sexually unfulfilled. For example, it was normal while growing up for boys to lie about love to get sex and for girls to lie about sex to get love. A teenage girl would give her boyfriend the impression she enjoyed sex much more than she actually did. Why? Because he told her he loved her and she wanted to show her appreciation by returning the love through her enjoyment of sex. Boys were left with the impression that good sexual performance is what's needed to prove their love to their girlfriends.

These boys grew up into men who believed that a girl who shows intimacy is definitely ready for sex.

"I just can't understand women," said Berkley, an industrial mechanic. "My wife gets nice and cuddly as if she is really in the mood. When I start to make my moves, she pulls away as if I was bothering her. It was not always like this, though. There was a time when all I had to do was touch her and she was ready. Now it seems she avoids me like the plague; it's as if she is no longer interested in sex. Or maybe I am doing something wrong."

Some men believe women lose their desire to actively participate in sex after marriage, after they have had their children, or as they grow older. Some even say a woman's sex drive is less than that of a man. And it's for these reasons they believe that women find excuses to avoid having sex with their husbands or mates. "Not tonight. I've got a headache" are familiar words to many husbands.

But is this true? Could it be that women eventually lose their desire to participate in sex? Not likely.

Biologically, human females are the sexiest beings alive. Women are unique in this respect; they can have sex any time, whether in or out of their mating season. If she chooses, a woman can have sex with multiple partners for many hours at a time whether day or night, and even during pregnancy. Many women are capable of multiple orgasms. So far there is no scientific evidence to prove that any other female in the animal species possesses this capability. For most other females in the animal kingdom, sex is limited to periods of fertility, and sex is usually tied in with their reproductive cycles.

So why do women say no to sex when they might like to say yes? Because a woman's ultimate goal is to love and nurture. Inherent in a woman psyche is the need to ensure the continuation of the species. She attracts a man with her sexuality, but once she connects with a man, she then wants to nurture him and perhaps create a family. [55]

But before she consents to having sex with him, she wants to be certain the man's intentions are similar to her own. "Does he want a life with me, or does he only want sex?"

That sounds reasonable, but why does the problem still exist even after marriage? What is it about the state of marriage that causes a change in women's attitude toward sex? As Terrence, age 38, asked "Why does marriage sometimes seem to be the best method of birth control there is?" The answer lies in the roots of relationships between men and women.

Sex and courtship

During courtship, a woman may be more receptive to sex because she believes that her partner loves and cares for her. And in most cases, she is right. The novelty of exploring the unknown is infatuating to a man. He feels that he is falling in love, a feeling difficult to hide while it's actually happening. This is the time when his actions toward his mate are spontaneous. He may suddenly get the urge to send flowers or buy her a thoughtful gift. The woman feels loved, which can make her emotionally ready for sex.

This period forms a memorable part of the courtship and later the relationship. Both parties would most likely remember it as a high point in their affair. The woman may imagine a future relationship of pure bliss. The man may remember this as the time when he succeeded in winning the love of the woman he truly wanted. As the relationship progresses and the man and the woman become more familiar with each other, the situation can change. For the man, the novelty and excitement associated with the chase diminishes after the conquest. And even though he may still be in love, he may lose the urge to express his love with the same spontaneity as he did before.

The woman will no doubt observe a change in her mate's actions and may interpret this change as a weakening of his love for her, thinking, "Maybe he doesn't love me like he used to." And since a woman's desire for sex is triggered by the quality of love she receives from her partner, she may become less receptive to her partner's sexual advances. Men who are out of touch with women's feelings find it difficult to understand a woman who behaves this way. A man asks, "What's going on here? I thought things were great between us."

And here we come face to face with the age-old battle between men and women: Men wanting more sex and women needing more love. The woman reminisces about the period in her life when she experienced blissful love with her partner. And the man recalls the time when his partner was receptive to sex and totally enjoyed it. Both parties longing to return to the happiness they once knew which, in many cases, turns out to be no easy task. The woman does not get the love she needs to trigger her desire to have sex, and the man does not get the sex he needs to express his love and intimacy for her. Here we arrive at a catch 22, which results in total physical and emotional frustration for them both.

But why don't they just talk about it. Why not just bring it out and openly discuss it? Seems logical, but it seldom happens. Why? Because of the training and experiences most people received from childhood. Parents taught their daughters that when a man loves a woman, he shows it by his actions; a woman does not need to ask. So by allowing a man to prove his love, a woman can judge whether the love she is receiving is real and not just another way of getting her into the sack. But why is a woman so obsessed with love as if her life depended on it? One reason is because she possesses the genes of her ancestors, who at some time in history, depended on love for their very survival.

In their book, *Why Men Don't Get Enough Sex & Women don't Get Enough Love*. Jonathan Kramer, Ph.D., and Diane Dunaway observe that, over the centuries, women have learned to control their sexuality. [56] Unlike men who want sex for the pure satisfaction of sex, women learned to let their desires for sex to be triggered only by certain circumstances. She has to be reasonably certain that her sexual partner is interested in her not only for sex, but he must also be capable and willing to make a commitment to love and care for her. To a woman, it became necessary to forgo her passions to enjoy sex until she feels a sense of security with her partner.

Today, this has become a key area of conflict between men and women. It has become a case of one-upmanship. The woman is on constant guard to ensure the man does not get sex without a commitment; if he does, he wins. If she is able to secure a commitment before or even after sex, she wins. And this is why we're in a constant battle of the sexes.

To better understand the complexities of sexual relationships between women and men, let's take a journey back in time.

Insight into a woman's psyche

For generations, psychologists have attempted to understand how a woman's mind works. The feminine psyche has always been associated with some sort of mystery. But if we were to look back far enough in history, we would see that, as with all life forms, biological, anthropological, and social forces account for who women are today.

Understanding how these evolutionary forces work provides insight into how they can and did shape present behavior. It's all in the genes.

Genes are formed from our DNA and are responsible for the inherent characteristics that distinguish one individual from another. Because our ancestor's genes have been passed on to us, we will possess most of their mental and physical characteristics.

Our brains have been designed by genetic evolution. This means that as human practices, customs, and behavior changed over centuries and generations, our brains were modified to adapt to these changes. For example, scientists suggest that if little by little for the next thousands of generations, the earth becomes immersed in water, the respiratory systems of future generations will be adapted to breathing under water. [57] With this in mind, we can see how the events that took place thousands of years ago still affect our present-day behavioral patterns.

A time of peace and tranquility over 6,000 years ago

There was a time in history when women were adored for their ability to produce and nurture life; motherhood was valued highly. Riane Eisler in her book *The Chalice and the Blade* refers to a goddess-based culture that existed in the Paleolithic period, also called the Old Stone Age, more than 6,000 years ago. [58] Men had great respect for women and were honored to offer their skills as hunters and gatherers to provide the food and security necessary for their mutual survival. These were times when men and women lived in peace and harmony with each other. Men freely expressed their love and women freely expressed their sexuality. There was no mention of any frustration between men and women about not enough sex and not enough love. These conflicts simply did not exist.

A man's power was measured by his skill as a hunter and provider; the more aggressive the man, the more skillful he was as a hunter. Violence among men in these times was rare and even when present, did not usually result in murder. Centuries passed in which people lived in well-organized tribes and enjoyed cooperation with each other. Then something happened that caused a drastic change in the history of mankind.

Shift to agricultural society

About 6,000 years ago at the beginning of the Neolithic period, mankind shifted away from hunting and gathering and concentrated on agriculture as a means of survival. This was an era when people learned to grow and harvest crops and to identify the most fertile lands close to water where crops can flourish. This began in the areas now known as Greece, Italy, and other parts of Europe. This new prosperity lasted for hundreds of years until some tribes figured out it was easier to steal from others than to produce their own crops. Of course, then people had to protect themselves and their communities. This new development produced generations of men who had to learn to defend themselves by killing their fellow men. New behavioral patterns had to be developed. Instead of learning hunting and gathering skills, men also had to be trained in preparation for war. [59]

Now instead of a peaceful existence, men had to learn to kill or be killed if they were to survive. This fact marked an evolutionary change in men; tender emotions had to be put aside in readiness for battle. For generations, men's energies were channeled in the direction of training and preparation of implements of violence. In time, generations of men were born in violence and encouraged to suppress tender emotions. The strongest and most capable of eliminating the enemy were the ones who survived. It's ironic to observe that, in earlier generations, power was measured by the ability to give and protect life. During this era, a man's power was measured by his ability to take life. Men were forced to suppress their emotions of consideration, tenderness, and compassion if they were to be competent warriors. [60]

A consequence of all this was that men became separated from a part of themselves, the part which enabled them to freely love their land, their fellow men, and their families. The ability to love, though not completely lost, became buried deep in their psyches. To access such emotions, a man had to delve deeply into himself, unlike before when these emotions were a dominant part of his makeup. To put it simply, men were separated from their ability to love freely.

Women continued to shoulder the responsibility of nurturing their families, but now had to be protected from the enemy. An attacking tribe would swoop down on a village, murder women and children, and make off with whatever surplus of crops they could find. Now, more that ever, women and children needed a man not only as a provider of food but also as a protector.

It's easy to see why the most powerful warriors would be the most capable protectors and would be in greatest demand. Unfortunately, the more aggressive the man, the less capable he was of compassion and less likely to show emotions. But women were attracted to such men instinctively because the presence, of a strong man in a woman's life increased her chances of survival. Its remarkable how dominant and far-reaching is the effect of our genetic makeup.

Today, 6,000 years later, even though women do not need protection from men, many women are still instinctively attracted to aggressive men. Women marry these men knowing they are less likely to show tenderness and intimacy. We have all heard of cases where "bad boys" are still a turn on for many women.

Imagine a generation of men forced to live by the sword. The show of any tender emotions would tell his enemy he is weak. Any hesitation to kill the enemy could result in his own death. If a man loses a brother or friend in battle, instead of lingering in mourning, he has to find the strength to move on with his agenda. Losing control of his emotions at that time could endanger not only himself but also his fellow warriors. A man had to be dominant in his dealings with other men in order to gain respect.

Now that the focus of power lie in a man's strength, men began to exercise their power by dominating others. And as we have learned from history, "absolute power corrupts absolutely." The equitable relationship that men and women enjoyed no longer existed. Whereas in the past, women were adored and respected for their power to bring forth and nurture life, now they were seen as objects of convenience for men. Some historians referred to this period as one of sexual enslavement for women. Men made laws to control women's sexuality, which stated, "Offer your sexuality to me and only me. [61] Give me as many children as you can so that I can increase my workforce. If you refuse, I will not protect you." One of the principal reasons man demanded fidelity from his woman was that he had to be certain he would be the biological father for all her children. This way he could count on their loyalty.

What choices did a woman have? She was not strong enough to defend herself, so she bartered her independence and sexuality for protection. She became the man's possession. This new social revolution produced women who, over time and generations, adapted their lifestyles to please their male masters. This period marked a very important milestone in the history of mankind. Scientists have identified these events as being directly responsible for the evolution of the unique trait that women possess, i.e., the ability to be constantly receptive to sex. Dr.

Helen Fisher New York Academy of Science noted that prehistoric women's sexuality evolved to its unique level of constant availability to keep men nearby in times of violence. [62]

Movement from peace to violence

Some anthropologists have speculated that, at some time in the human evolution, men naturally became superior to women, but so far there has been no hard evidence to support this. This historical shift from peace to violence coupled with the need to survive was wholly responsible for the male's dominance over females, not some natural process of evolution. It is, however, important to look at the other side of the coin.

One might blame men for what took place in prehistoric times, but we must consider that men had no choice. If they did, they would have probably taken the peaceful route. Some, not all men, became violent, and violence breeds violence. When one man takes up arms, others are forced to follow suit or die. The super powers of today's world know this only too well. For this reason, they maintain constant collaboration with each other to maintain control over the spread of nuclear weapons. A nuclear first strike today by any nation against another could result in a drastic change to human existence as we know it today.

Warriors also needed love

After a day on the battlefield, a warrior needed a moment of peace and tranquility to reconnect with his inner self. Even in times of peace, he had to train himself to be in a constant state of readiness for combat. Inherent in a man's training is the ability to be self-sufficient. He must be able to withstand extreme hardships without losing his ability to function effectively. At the same time, he also learned to depend only on himself. But the desire to bond with another human is a powerful force that we simply cannot suppress. According to Helen Fisher, PhD., bonding is deeply engraved in the human psyche. [63]

It is important to examine the powerful sexual pull that draws a man to a woman. Many men see sex as a form of self-satisfaction and, to some extent, a form of recreation. But according to psychologists, sexual desire aims at the joining of two people emotionally and is by no means only a physically satisfying experience. Sex brings two people together from a position of loneliness and the need to connect with another. [64]

So while a man struggles to maintain his armor of separateness, he cannot escape the longing to make that connection with another human. Women, by their inherent nature, provide the link a man needs to reconnect to his inner self.

A man's need for a woman has never changed. He has always needed love, sex, and companionship. Now more than ever, he needed a woman who, by her mere presence, returns him to a state of tranquility; that special place where he can escape the horrors of war and the extreme stress of being a man in difficult times. A woman's natural desire to love and nurture became the ticket to her survival. Of course, there was competition for the most eligible men. These were the men who were most capable as providers and protectors of the women and their children.

Most likely a woman had to turn on her charm as both a giver and a recipient of love, a caretaker and an appetizing sexual partner. By satisfying most of her man's needs, a woman could feel secure that the man will be comfortable and happy, and want to remain close to her. Over time, women grew to love and accept their roles as caretakers of their men. Some anthropologists believe that, apart from the need to survive, women wanted to heal men by reconnecting them to their inner self - a task which has taken hundreds of generations and is still not yet completed.

Why can't men say "I love you"?

Even though men wanted to reconnect with their tender emotional selves, generations of training have prevented them from doing so. This is understandable. Remember, men needed to maintain an image of aggressiveness, ruthlessness, power, and independence if they were to be victorious against their enemies. Even in the presence of their women, they instinctively did not let down their guard. Their hearts said yes but their training and conditioning said no. The Bible referred to the historical significance of events that took place in the Garden of Eden long ago when Eve seduced Adam into partaking of the forbidden fruit. It also tells the mythical account of betrayal when Delilah cut off Samson's hair causing him to lose his enormous strength, then delivered him to the Philistines. Even today, these and other historical references serve as a reminder to men of the consequences of falling in love.

So men sought to protect themselves by covering up their feelings of love. They learned to be cool and calm, and to control certain emotions, expressing them only under certain circumstances. In short, men were taught to keep their heads on. What they could not suppress, however, was their physical need for sex. And since sex was a part of love anyway, men felt they could achieve emotional bonding with women through sex alone.

Subsequent generations of men evolved believing that a man's desire to have sex with a woman is enough to demonstrate his love for a woman. A man felt she could measure the intensity of his love by his desire to have sex with her.

That was then. So why do men continue to act this way hundreds of years afterward? Because in today's world, the situation that existed then has not changed very much. No century in the history of mankind has past where men were not engaged in war. Closer to home, are the Korean, Vietnam, Bosnian, and most recently Afghanistan wars. Even today, men are required to maintain a state of alertness.

But even in times of peace, a man cannot afford the luxury of letting his guard down; the world is a very competitive place. While in the past, men's training prepared them for war, today they have to be ready for the fierce competition that exists in the world of commerce. For example, every present-day CEO knows he/she has to maintain a constant state of vigilance and alertness to secure market share for the corporation he represents. Instead of spears and clubs, people have to design automobiles, airports, and computer software. Instead of depending on physical strength to kill an animal for food, men and women today have to find ways to earn money.

The game is survival

Again we acknowledge the dominance of our ancestral genes. Our ancestors struggled to attain power because power meant they were less vulnerable to attack from their enemies. This fact alone increased their chances of survival. In today's society, power and status mean a man would have access to a wider selection of women hence, more possibilities for survival of the species. Remarkable! In his book *On Human Nature*, Edward Wilson identified a founder of a block of villages who fathered 45 children by eight wives. By the time his sons had children, 75% of the village population were his descendants. [65]

The drive to succeed

It has been said that after sex, success is the most important thing to men. They work long hours, travel half way around the world, and endure whatever hardships necessary to increase their chances of success. A man would not be considered worthwhile unless he could show the world he is able to earn a good income, buy a nice house, and drive a nice car. Behavioral scientists believe one of the reasons men put all their effort into being successful is because they have only a few ways to show their value. Whereas a woman could be a mother, a wife, or a successful career person (many areas to show her self-worth), most of a man's perceived value comes from success in the outer world. Being a good father and considerate husband are also important, but many still associate these qualities with material achievements. Mary, 36, a fashion designer, said "I feel good when my partner buys me expensive romantic gifts, but I would feel better if I knew he really could afford them."

Another reason for a man's relentless drive to succeed is that the satisfaction derived from material success is usually short lived. A man may achieve great levels of success but still continue to strive to achieve more. He believes he will arrive at a point when he will be fully contented, only to be disappointed if this does not happen.

Neil, 46, is a businessman who finally achieved what he considered ultimate success. He sold his company to a large business conglomerate. His life's goal was to bring his business to such a level of productivity that a larger company would want to acquire it. He finally did it. Financially, he was set for life. Now he had time and the freedom to do whatever he wanted. He spent the most part of a year traveling and doing all the things he always dreamed about.

But within two years, Neil was in a state of chronic depression. His life consisted mostly of gambling and alcohol abuse. Luckily for him, he sought professional treatment and was able to avoid complete disaster in his life. Neil experienced a period of depression because he expected to be rewarded after having achieved his goal. Even though he might not have known exactly how, he thought that in some way his life would dramatically change for the better. When this did not happen, he felt cheated and experienced a feeling of emptiness inside.

Are men capable of love?

Sometimes men's drive for success causes them to allocate more priority to material achievements than to their women. Of course, the more they succeed, the happier their wives will be, or so they may believe. A man may reason, "Maybe I am not spending enough time to talk to or listen to her as she would like, but I bet she'll sing a different tune when I buy her the dream house, or that nice diamond she wants."

Even today, it is still difficult for men to express emotions of love for the reasons described earlier. This, however, does not mean that men cannot or do not love. Perhaps if women and men were to understand the difference between male love and female love, they may see an end to the age-old battle of the sexes.

What can men do to have sex with their wives more often?

One of the principal reasons a woman says no to sex is because she is mentally and physically tired. The misconception about housework being a breeze is difficult to erase from men's minds. Even though we are beginning to see signs of changes in the modern man, a great many continue to practice the traditional rules.

Here's why this situation persists.

While growing up, men saw their fathers being waited on by their mothers. Most mothers made it clear to their sons that it's not manly to do housework, and that to gain respect from their future wives, they have to maintain their manly position in their homes. This position has become obsolete in many cases. Modern women pay their own bills and are not willing to wait on men at the end of the day.

Girls were also students of the same teaching, and as adults some of them accepted the traditional role as housewife. Even today, some women say they welcome their husband's help sometimes, but they prefer to take total responsibility for housework. Although such women are by no means in the majority, they do exist. By their nature, women are nurturers but this does not mean that they are servants. They may be comfortable with their roles as caretakers of their families, but sometimes the responsibilities become overwhelming. Women do need help and more so when they are saddled with the additional responsibility of working outside the home.

The traditional woman may not ask her man for help, not wanting to belittle him by asking him to do what society considers "woman's work." Also, the woman might feel she is treading on thin ice by asking him to. Why? Because instinctively a woman may have learned that, by asking a man to do more, he may assume she feels he is not doing enough. And she may not be wrong; most men see the task of providing for their families as difficult, but they accept it as their responsibility. They believe their woman should appreciate their efforts. Men say, "Yes, she can complain about the small problems at home with the kids, but I have to make sure that there is enough money to keep us going," or words to that effect.

But by not asking for help, the man may assume she does not need it. So he sits in front of the TV and even makes additional requests of the woman. "Honey, would you mind calling the doctor to make me an appointment?" Now imagine how infuriating this could be to the woman.

The woman expects her man to understand her situation and is surprised when he doesn't. She reasons, "How inconsiderate of him. He sees I am very busy; he makes no effort to assist me; he asks me to do more and then still expects me to be nice and ready for sex at bedtime. Yeah- right."

How men can improve the situation

1. Men, let your woman know you are aware she is under tremendous pressure and offer to help wherever you can.

Pay close attention to her activities in the home. Volunteer to do the housework once in a while when you get home from work. You might be surprised to learn that housework is no easy task.

2. Pick the chores you know she dislikes doing and do them for her. There are some household chores that some women do not enjoy doing, but they do them anyway because they feel it's their duty. For example, clean up after a party. She will appreciate it.

3. Invite her to dinner away from the house but also make arrangements to take care of pending household chores. Women often complain. "Sure he wants to take me to dinner and I do enjoy eating out once in a while, but what good is that if I have to come back to an untidy house and dirty dishes?"

4. Show her you appreciate her efforts by telling her so. Knowing her man values her efforts revitalizes a woman even if she is stressed. She may not only find new energy to complete her task, but she may also enjoy it.

5. Tell her that you love her. For many guys, this is a big one; I've heard all kinds of excuses on this one, like saying, "I am not the emotional type." By my actions, she should know that I love her." "I've stayed married to her for 12 years, didn't I?" But, guys remember that women do want to hear the words. Just as important are the actions that go with the words. Call her in the middle of the day to let her know that you are thinking about her. Let her know how much you admire the things she does. You may like the way she dresses, how she handles her job, how she shows consideration for others. Tell her so.

Seize every opportunity to let her know how valuable she is to you. Very few things make a woman feel loved as when she knows you are a source of joy and happiness in her life.

6. Keep the courtship going. Surprising as it may seem, many men still believe that once the initial courtship is over and they succeed in winning the woman, the need for further courtship is no longer a priority. Then they wonder why their women are not turned on by their sexual advances. Both men and women need romance. They need to be assured their partners still find them attractive and desirable. This way, they can feel they are still loved. Use your imagination to come up with some creative ideas to do something sweet for your mate. Don't feel you have to do something costly, the most thoughtful and romantic things cost little or nothing.

7. Get to know her even better. Psychologists say that the excitement of getting to know someone diminishes and subsequently disappears after you feel you sufficiently know the person. Most often, people have not scratched the surface when it comes to knowing someone. If, in fact, you were to take time to learn about your partner, you may be surprised to discover how truly exciting he/she can be. [66]

Also, guys, take time to study your woman. Look for subtle things that get her interest. Look into her eyes, a good source of body language. Eye contact is a good way of knowing if someone is attracted to you. It worked while we were courting; let's keep the romance alive if we want to keep our women happy. When a woman is happy, pleasing her man becomes her pleasure.

8. Focus more on intimacy rather than sex. Many women say they prefer to cuddle in bed and sometimes cuddling can put them in the mood. So set her alarm clock to go off half an hour before the regular time. This way you can have time for some early morning cuddling; it can do wonders for her day.

Turning off the lights and getting down to business is not always the best approach. Talk to her; don't be timid to talk about sex. Women are suspicious of the intentions of a guy who never talks about sex. "Maybe there is no love, only sexual desires," they might think. Remember, women like to communicate their feelings of love and would like that their partners do the same. Women experience a feeling of emptiness if they are unable to get this communication from their mates. Contrary to the belief of some misguided men, women seek extramarital affairs out of the need for communication rather than sex. According to an Oasis Mayo Clinic study, the more often a woman was able to freely discuss sex with her partner, the more satisfying was her sex life, her marriage, and her general happiness. [67]

To many men, this information is not new. But partly because of the reasons explained earlier and constant misinformation by the media, this conflict between men and women still exist. What some men may not realize is how crucial it is to constantly nurture and satisfy the emotional needs of a woman. When men understand this key element in a sexual relationship, they will go that extra mile if it means having the sexual relationship they want. Perhaps there will come a time when men no longer complain about not getting enough.

Chapter Twelve
Sharing intimacy

All you need is love

It's no accident that John Lennon's words have stuck in the minds of people everywhere. But even before we heard John Lennon or the Beatles, we were told that love conquers all. And even if you are not from that era, artists like Celine Dion today constantly remind us of *The Power of Love.*

However, many who believe that a happy and successful relationship automatically follows when a strong and passionate love connection exists between two people often misinterpret this message. Life's experiences continue to teach us that although love can serve as a solid base upon which to build a successful relationship, by itself, it offers no guarantee. Clearly we have seen that love is not enough.

Is the honeymoon over?

At the first sign of marital problems between newlyweds or other couples who have recently entered a relationship, we often hear people say, "Ah… the honeymoon is over."

Today, people have come to expect relationships to be short-lived. And when we look at statistics that tell us the average lifespan of first marriages is about three years, it's no wonder even the couples themselves in a relationship are sometimes not surprised when their relationship ends prematurely.

But it does not have to be this way. And as people who enjoy blissful relationships would tell you, their honeymoon is not over. So why is it that some people enjoy blissful relationships while others don't?

Let's look at what men and women have in mind when they embark on a search for a partner. Most people seek an intimate connection with someone, a deep connection in which they feel completely at ease with each other and don't have to hide themselves for fear their partner will criticize or reject them.

If you're in this kind of relationship, you can drop your mask and don't have to play games. You can relax because you have accepted who you are and you know that your partner loves you the way you are. Imagine, your mate knows all of you, your strengths, your weaknesses, your fears and shortcomings, how you look when you are at your worst, and how you behave when you are in your worst mood. Your partner knows you and says, "I see you; I know everything about you, I love you just the way you are." Yes, this is what true intimacy and romantic love is all about.

But some people mistakenly believe this stage of intimacy comes automatically when two people fall in love. It does not happen that way; you have to make a conscious effort to open the door to your heart so that love can come in. Let's look at the case of Janice, a 37-year-old housewife.

Two years after divorcing her husband of 12 years, Janice met and started dating Donald a 42-year-old businessman who immediately fell for her. She proceeded cautiously with Donald. She found it extremely difficult to trust another man; because the relationship with her husband ended on a bitter note.

But Donald has treated her special, being gentle, caring, and patient with her. She has long closed the door on the relationship she had with her husband so there is no longing to return there. For these reasons, she cannot understand why she has not fallen head over heels in love with Donald. She said, "Things are not so bad. I feel comfortable with Donald and he continues to be patient with me, so why am I not hearing the chimes of bells? Is there something wrong with me?"

For reasons she does not understand, Janice has not opened her heart to Donald. And one thing is certain. Until she consciously opens her heart to the love he is sending, she will continue to feel the emptiness she experienced in her marriage.

What prevents people from opening their hearts to love?

For a long time, psychoanalysts have identified the problem of **self-alienation** in humans. [68] This is a condition exhibited by people who have lost touch with their true feelings. They are never sure what represents reality to them. This causes people to act unconsciously to whatever motivates them. They are not certain if their actions are guided by their true feelings or by outside influences. How does this happen?

Most people have been conditioned from childhood to suppress their feelings. On a visit to a friend's house, I remember seeing his young daughter Nancy came running into the living room screaming at the top of her voice when she heard that her favorite uncle had come to visit. With the same excitement, she leaped into her uncle's arms. It was clear how thrilled she was to see him.

Later, I overheard her mother scolding her. "You know, young ladies do not behave that way, running and screaming like that. You can go to your uncle and say 'How are you, it's nice to see you.'"

Most men remember the pain of being hurt while playing as a child. The natural reaction of a child, experiencing pain is to cry. His father would tell him that boys don't cry. As a boy grows older, he is reminded by his peers that men are not supposed to show emotions

If, for example, a boy develops a flare for the arts and expresses a desire to take ballet classes, his mates will likely call him a sissy or a wimp.

With the desire to please her mother and as a reward for being loved, girls like Nancy will try to suppress her excitement and be more ladylike. Boys will hide their emotions so their peers will accept them. So by the time these children become adults, they might have forgotten or completely lost the desire to express the emotions they possessed as children. "If you don't use it, you loose it." But these feelings and emotions don't go away. They are a part of you and will always remain that way. "A leopard never loses his spots"

In addition to direct teaching, psychologists have noted that children learn by example. Their subconscious minds are constantly absorbing the lessons learned by the actions of their parents and the people around them. A boy who observes his father as the dominant figure in his household may believe a man must always maintain his superiority to a woman in a relationship. And people who practice certain religions teach their children that certain thoughts and emotions are evil, and should be purged from their minds.

All of these factors cause confusion in the mind of a child; he or she begins life in touch with his or her natural feelings, and later learns that certain emotions are not acceptable. Yet these emotions are a part of his or her personality. What is the solution for the child?

The child builds into his/her personality a state of unconsciousness as a form of coping and protection against emotions, which are perceived as threatening to his/her safety or self-esteem. The results of this produce humans who base their value system on whatever prompts them or seems socially acceptable at the moment, instead of letting their spontaneous emotions be their guide. Depending on her upbringing, a woman may suppress her full expression of feeling during sex for fear she may shock her partner. So she goes along with whatever she believes is acceptable, thus denying herself true fulfillment in her sex life. She may even blame her mate for her lack of sexual fulfillment.

To achieve intimacy in your relationship, both you and your partner must consciously agree to share your true selves with each other. Your partner must know who you truly are so he/she can love the real you. But before this can happen, you have to know the real you. You have to know what you honestly feel. You have to remove the layers of resistance which conceal buried or repressed emotions so that these emotions can surface and be integrated into your present system. The good news is that many people have been successful in reclaiming their disowned emotions.

Reclaiming suppressed or disowned parts of yourself

When people say they are trying to find themselves, they are sometimes referring to the parts of their psyche that may have been disowned by them a long time ago. Sometimes the real you that is deeply buried wants to surface, if only you would allow it to do so. But for many people, this is not easy. They are submerged parts of the self that will rise to a conscious level, producing anxiety and even fear. You may wonder, "Would people think less of me when they find out what my true feelings are?" "If my mate discovers that I sometimes cry, would she still respect me as a man?" Or "Would I receive the same attention and care from men if they find out that I am not as helpless as they thought?"

I know a lady who has always been possessed by the urge to fix things. If, for example, she was out on a date and the car developed problems, she would be shoulder to shoulder with her date trying to fix it. After a while, she had to restrain herself from offering to fix mechanical things in the presence of men because she found out most men felt uncomfortable in her company. Now that she pretends to be helpless around men, she finds she is being asked out on dates more frequently.

How do you rediscover and reclaim disowned parts of yourself?

1. Listen to your inner voice. Take some quiet time alone to listen to your thoughts and notice your spontaneous actions. Why? Because your spontaneous thoughts and actions determine who you really are. You may modify your actions when in the company of others, but you and only you will know your true thoughts. Also, it may be helpful to keep a journal. There, you can record your thoughts and insights because it's easy to forget them when you get bogged down with outside influences. You may find it difficult to find quiet time in your busy day, but as little as 15 minutes in a quiet place should be enough.

2. Honestly pay attention to your actions. Never mind what you say to other people. Guide yourself by your own actions. You may lead others to believe, for example, that you are ruthless when it comes to charging for your professional services, but you perform the same services for free at the local community center. Or, it may appear that you like to dress elegantly when you feel more comfortable in a t-shirt and jeans.

3. Seek professional help. Some people may find it difficult to reclaim their disowned and suppressed emotions by themselves. In such cases it is wise to consult a psychotherapist or other professional who can guide you through the process. Other ways exist, too.

The *Option Method* was created by Bruce Di Marsico. This is a simple questioning method that helps people to reveal to themselves how they are governed by their own belief systems. The *Option Method* has received much attention in recent times. Many people claim it has assisted them in finding the source of their unhappiness. The following is an article published by Jennifer Hautman of the *Option Method Network.*

Why the Option Method works: by Jennifer Hautman, inspired by Mandy Evans' audio cassette 'Choosing happiness', and reprinted with permission.

Option Method dialogues go to the very core and centre of all unhappiness, your beliefs. The process gives you the opportunity to first see your beliefs. They allow you to investigate them to see whether they are serving you in your life. The hundreds of thousands of beliefs that make up your belief systems may have been acquired long ago from parents, teachers, society, etc., yet are still operating as the source for your feelings and actions in the present.

The Option Method is unique in that it offers the opportunity, sometimes for the first time, to look at and review these beliefs head on, in black and white, and with your eyes wide open. Often self-defeating beliefs crumble under the scrutiny of investigation. Once you change a limiting belief, what results can appear miraculous, but there is nothing mysterious about it.

Without the limiting beliefs, you are free to experience powerful, life-changing results. Issues and challenges that caused years of discomfort can often be dropped with ease.

Why is it so easy?

Imagine you work in an office with ten other people. In the foyer, which you pass through each day, there is a 12 x 12-foot area rug. The receptionist warned you the first time you came in the office about a big hole in the floor under the rug and to stay clear of it. It was dangerous. You've now been working for this company for two years. The rug and hole have become a natural fixture to the office. The people who work there just know to give that area of the building a wide girth. Walking in from lunch, you and your co-worker don't miss a beat in your conversation as you walk around the rug. You don't even think about it much anymore.

You've had discussions with other co-workers about why the owner doesn't fix the hole, or at least put up a barrier with signs until it's fixed. There have been theories proposed like the owner doesn't care because he doesn't come in the office, that the business isn't doing well and he can't afford to fix it. Not impeding your work, you accept the hole as a "necessary evil" for working for the company.

Then one day, a new employee gets curious and pulls back the carpeting. He wants to see the hole. To his surprise, there is no hole!! He calls to everyone to come and see. As you all stand around looking at where the hole was supposed to be, you try and figure out why you all believed the hole was there in the first place. Who started this hole (whole?) mythology?!?

As it turns out, the owner had the hole fixed the weekend following the damage, but didn't inform the employees. "Just like management," one employee says, "they don't tell us anything." You each take a turn tentatively stepping on the floor where there was supposed to be a hole. You laugh as each person tests the area by jumping and dancing on "the hole." It's as solid as a rock. You're surprised and amazed.

After some discussion, you eventually make your way back to work. The next day when you enter the office, you walk around the rug. You chuckle to yourself thinking "old habits," then turn and walk over the rug to your office. With each passing day, you forget all about the hole and think nothing of where you walk.

Was it difficult to walk on the rug once you saw there was no hole? Did you need to go through years of therapy in order to do so? Did you need to analyze your childhood? Heal any wounds? Release your anger? No, you just walked on it. No big deal. Your actions and experience naturally changed once you knew there was no hole there.

This is how it works with beliefs. Changing what you believe changes your behaviors and feelings. You no longer make a circle around the rug. You no longer warn new people. You no longer look at the rug and think, "Why doesn't someone do something about that." All because your belief about the hole has changed. It can be that easy.

You can practice the option method by yourself or have an option practitioner assist you through the dialogue questions for the first times anyway. Contact the Option Network at http://optionmethodnetwork.com/practitioners.htm for more information.

When you are free to honestly know what you feel, you can then share these feelings with the one you love. This is not to say that you have to share every last detail about yourself and your feelings with your mate: even in the most intimate relationship, judgment should prevail. Some thoughts and perceptions are sometimes better kept to yourself. But there are certain emotions that affect your everyday life, and it is important for your partner to be intimately aware of such feelings and emotions.

Communicating feelings to each other

• Expressing fear

For some time, Dennis, a technician at a packaging company in Ohio, had been hearing rumors that his company may be closing down. The economic situation in the country had taken a downward turn and Dennis knew the packaging business usually suffers in a slow economy.

After 15 years with the company, Dennis was worried that he could suddenly find himself out of a job. His wife Elizabeth noticed he has not been himself lately; he would lie in bed gazing at the ceiling. When she asked him if something was the matter, he would say that everything was all right. She accepted this at first, but as the days went by, she noticed that Dennis seemed uneasy and the simplest thing would upset him. She insisted that he tell her what was bothering him. Dennis became defensive and a quarrel developed. One thing led to another and the fighting between them lasted for weeks. Their marriage began to deteriorate so Elizabeth decided to seek help from a marriage counselor. The counselor requested to see them both, but Dennis was reluctant to do so. As the situation in their marriage became worse, he finally agreed to see the therapist.

It came out after a few sessions that Dennis was overtaken by the fear of losing his job. He had imagined himself in financial difficulties and dreaded the thought of losing their home. He did not want to tell his wife about his fears because he did not want her to worry. He believed that "he is the man" and it's his responsibility to maintain his family.

The marriage counselor helped Dennis and his wife by giving them some suggestions on how to deal with the situation, and Dennis was able to overcome some of his anxieties.

Consider what might have happened if Elizabeth did not

take the initiative to seek professional help. The fighting between this couple could have developed into serious problems.

Many of us associate fear with weakness. We feel a sense of humiliation if others find out that we are afraid. Most men like to give the impression that they are bold and fearless, and people have come to expect men to act that way. It's always an amusement for the attendants in the doctor's office when I tell them I am afraid of injections. They always comment, "Come on. A big guy like you can't be afraid of this small needle."

It may be okay to show a lack of fear in certain situations, (like when you're coaching others) but it helps to let your mate know when you are afraid. Sometimes simply talking about your fear with your partner can help overcome it. And sometimes the mere listening to your partner can give them the strength to act against his/her fear.

Failing to express your true emotions to your mate can sometimes cause misunderstandings, which may develop into serious problems in your relationship. I think of a man who could not understand why his wife becomes jealous when he flirts with other women at a party. "I don't see her point; she knows I love her yet she gets extremely jealous when I dance with other women. She knows that I'm not going anywhere, but I enjoy having a good time when I'm at a party." Every time they go out to a party, she gives him the silent treatment for days afterward, and this has caused some tension in their relationship.

This woman's jealousy results from fear of losing her husband to another woman. It may be true he has no intention of running off with another, but that does not eliminate his wife's fear. As a woman, she is reluctant to express this fear to her husband, thinking he may believe she lacks self-confidence. She therefore takes the stand that, as his wife, he ought not to put her through what she considers an embarrassment in public. Her husband, on the other hand, misinterprets her feelings and believes that she is just a spoiled sport.

If the woman was to express her true feelings to her husband, and say to him, "You know honey, I know that you love me and I know that you are not in the market for another woman, but for some reason I am fearful. I am terrified by visions of you leaving me. And it doesn't help when I see you having a good time with other women." If she was to confide in him that her feelings go deeper than petty jealousy, he may be able to better understand her preoccupation.

Anger: A natural reaction

When either you or your partner expresses anger, you are expressing an honest feeling, but this does not mean you no longer love each other.

Anger is a form of communication, which tells your partner your perception of what has happened or what was said. It is a normal and spontaneous reaction. But some of us choose to withhold our expression of anger, perhaps in an attempt to maintain peace and tranquility in our relationships. According to Dr. Constance McKenzie M.ED., MA, the more we withhold feelings instead of letting them out, the more likely we are to have an angry outburst as the pressure builds inside. [69]

Many of society's educators, parents, teachers, religious leaders, etc., teach that anger is a negative emotion that gets us into trouble and should not be expressed. They note that the momentary relief we may gain from impulsively expressing anger is not worth the possible negative consequences that can result. [70] We like to be good citizens, so we do our best not to show anger.

However, withholding your expression of anger may be okay in social gatherings, business meetings, etc., but can be a source of misunderstandings in a loving relationship. Why? Because in an intimate relationship, it is wise to know your mate's true feelings at all times. You honestly may not be aware of how your actions may hurt, belittle, or offend the ones you love. Sometimes it takes an expression of anger to get your attention.

Expressing anger, however, should not be confused with attacking your partner. "You are no different from my last husband/wife; I should have known you'll be like this." Or "You inconsiderate so and so. I know you did this so you can get back at me." Instead of communicating your feelings honestly, such expressions are designed to provoke an attack, like a declaration of war.

When someone who loves you perceives that your words or actions were intended to cause pain (in many cases mistakenly so), he/she reacts spontaneously and passionately. It is a reflex reaction. He/she cannot understand how someone with whom he/she shares such strong love and intimacy can intentionally hurt him/her.

Such a reaction indicates that true love does exist in the relationship, [71] and it should be viewed that way. Someone who is in a relationship for reasons of convenience and not necessarily for love may react in a similar situation with indifference or withhold expressing anger while planning revenge.

So in a loving relationship, allow your partner the freedom to express anger. Don't argue or fight back, but listen attentively while he/she vents angry feelings. If you constantly ignore, make light of, or fail to acknowledge your partner's anger, he/she may turn off and withdraw to himself/herself. This can begin a downward turn in your relationship.

The case of Monica and Robert provides a good example of how happy couples handle anger.

When Monica came home from work one evening, Robert had still not arrived; he gets home about an hour before Monica on most days. She didn't think much of it until she noticed it was after eleven o'clock and he had still not shown up. She telephoned his place of work where she learned that he had left hours ago. By 2:00 a.m., she was besides her self with worry. Robert had not yet come home nor had he called to say where he was.

At 3:30 a.m., she was on the phone to friends when he walked in the door. "What happened?" she asked. He casually told her that everything was okay and that he just decided to stay out for a while.

Monica erupted. "Why do you do this to me? I've been up all night sick with worry thinking that something terrible had happened to you. I was just about to call the police. Listen, I can't talk about this now. I'm going to bed, and I'll see you in the morning."

Monica gave a spontaneous response when she was satisfied that Robert was safe. It was triggered by passion caused by the love she had for her husband. However, she had to contain herself so she wouldn't be overcome by her own emotions. She withdrew and said, "I'll see you in the morning." Notice she did not attack nor attempt to abuse Robert in any way, and he did not detect aggression in her voice.

No doubt Robert would apologize to his wife later for being inconsiderate. But at the time, he chose to do nothing even though he may have been under stress. He understood it was necessary for Monica to vent her anger. Usually people don't react this way; they react with strong or abusive expressions, sparking a confrontation that develops into a win-lose or right-wrong situation. Under stress, people react in ways they may regret later.

Expressing happiness, love, and excitement

Just as it's important for lovers to communicate their negative emotions to each other, it is equally important to share happy and positive emotions as well. It may seem natural for people to want others to know when they are happy, but many couples are reluctant to openly express happiness to each other. Why?

A simple explanation is that if you don't trust someone, you will be afraid to expose your intimate feelings in his/her presence. "If I show my undying love and devotion to him, I will become his slave." Or "If she believes that I can't live without her, she will take advantage of me." But in a love relationship, this is a recipe for failure because intimacy and trust are vital ingredients for maintaining passion. How could you be in love with someone you cannot trust?

To share your life with someone does not mean only living under the same roof. It means sharing our inner feelings and processes, how you perceive things, what turns you on, what brings you happiness, what makes you sad, and what you fantasize about. All of these should be expressed so your partner can better understand who you are.

In a group session, a woman explained her husband's lack of excitement during sex. "Yes, he goes through the motions, but I never see any sign of excitement on his face. He says he is satisfied, but I don't see any evidence that this is so. It frustrates me and makes me feel inadequate; I think I am not turning him on." This is a source of torment for people in relationships with partners who have learned to suppress their excitement.

What inspiration and satisfaction we receive when we know

that we stimulate joy and excitement in our partner's life! And contrary to men's popular belief, sexual passion is also maintained by the feedback we receive when we stimulate excitement in our lovers and not only by our expert sexual performances.

The inspiration we receive from such feedback applies not only to sexual issues. The excitement I see on my wife's face when we visit historical sites encourages me to plan trips where we can include visits to such locations. And many of us can't wait to buy our lovers that vanilla ice cream sundae or that lobster dinner, which we know he/she would die for.

Unfortunately, however, many of us have been brought up to conceal this excitement. We have learned that, in order to appear grown up, we must contain our feelings of excitement. People will see us as being silly and childish if we get too excited. You may recognize this if, for instance, you caught someone off guard who is deeply involved in his or her music. You enter the room unexpectedly to find him/her dancing and performing, but at the first sign of intrusion, he/she abruptly stops the performance with a look of embarrassment.

Sometimes we want to express our excitement and let our partners know how much joy they have stimulated in us. But it is our partners who withdraw, making us believe it's best not to show such feelings, that some things are better left unexpressed.

How do we overcome this problem?

Dr. Gary A. Davis PhD, University of Wisconsin-Madison, have observed that creative people, artists, musicians, writers, etc., show some childlike qualities such as outbursts of excitement and lack of caution. [72] Some people may see such traits as immature. But this spontaneous outlook and reaction to life is necessary to maintain passion. If something turns you on, let it show, enjoy the moment. If you feel like screaming with excitement, go ahead. Who cares if someone might be listening? And if you find yourself afraid or embarrassed about expressing your emotions, make a conscious effort to accept that you are fearful or embarrassed. Don't fight it; accept it. Honestly let it come out in the open. Then you can be free to move on.

To know you is to love you

There is a wonderful feeling of satisfaction and security in a relationship when two lovers feel known and understood by each other.

When you truly love someone you would like to know and understand everything you can about that person's world. This is true for any relationship. Mothers often say to their children, "I know you like the back of my hand." This is easy to understand because of the deep intimate connection between mother and child.

Such intimate connection, however, should be no different between two people in a romantic love partnership. Brian Adams sang it in an upbeat tempo: "I want to know you like you know yourself," in his song "Inside Out."

People who enjoy blissful love relationships are intimately familiar with their partner's likes, dislikes, perceptions, joys, and stresses. They know what makes him/her happy or sad, what matters most or least in his/her life. Such people will be able to predict what their mates would do if they suddenly won the lottery. Or they could say how he/she would react, if that person's immediate boss just got fired from the company.

Of course, the opposite is true for relationships that are not functioning well. Here's an example. A woman came home, her face bursting with excitement. She said to her husband, "I've just won the ten million dollar lottery. Start packing." The husband, also overtaken with joy, rushed to the closet to select his luggage.

He hesitated, "What should I pack, should I pack for the mountains of for the beach?" The woman replied, "I don't care where you go; just get the heck out of here." Talk about being out of touch with your mate's feelings!

Stay connected

In the earlier stages of relationships, people eagerly want to learn as much as they can about their partner's world because falling in love is exciting. Remember the many hours on the telephone when you were getting to know each other? And the long conversations that kept you awake until the wee hours of the morning and in bed until midday on Sundays? Harvard psychiatrists Richard Schwartz and Jacqueline Olds, in their book Marriage in Motion explain that in a relationship two people are never at a standstill. They are either moving closer or further apart. When the movement is toward each other, they experience a state of joy and excitement in the relationship because of the novelty in discovering each other. [73]

But as they become more familiar with their mates, they become less enthusiastic about the discovery process. This does not necessarily mean that they have lost interest. Albert Ellis, PhD., says that excitement diminishes as curiosity about a mate is satisfied. People begin to feel they know their mates as well as they need to. But remember, as the world changes, so do perceptions, desires, and personal insights.

It is therefore necessary to keep the channels of communications open so you feel the desire to keep each other up to date with emotional developments in your lives. Also knowledge of each other's world comes in handy in times of turbulence in your relationship. For example, you may be experiencing pressures from in-laws and question where true loyalty lies. But you already know your mate's position on this subject; therefore you are better equipped to weather the storm. Intervention from well-intentioned but over-enthusiastic in-laws can be a major cause of quarrels between couples.

Tips on staying connected

1. Make time to catch up on what's happening in each other's lives.

No matter how busy you are, always take a moment to catch up on each other's day. For example, you are rushing to get ready to leave the house in the morning when your mate says, "I had a strange dream last night." Instead of saying, "Look I'm already late, I haven't got the time to listen right now," take a minute to hear at least some part of what your mate has to say. Then say, "That sounds real strange. Let's talk about this later when I get home. I want to hear more but I'm in a rush right now." Dreams may not be as important to you as to your partner, but by listening carefully, you can learn something about your mate's innermost thoughts. If you show no interest, your partner may withdraw and keep such matters to himself/herself in the future.

2. Make your relationship the highest priority.

To some people, this is easier said than done. Martin, an industrial steel worker, complains how tired he is at the end of the day. "Yes, she wants me to spend time talking and doing silly things to keep the relationship going. But I am more interested in using the time to make sure there is always money to cover the bills at the end of the month."

Karen is a human resource manager at a large company. Her job is satisfying, but she became scared when she thought it caused her to lose interest in sex. Her husband Ralph understood that she was under pressure at work but after six months of no sex, he, too, became anxious. They both agreed to seek professional help. "I knew I still loved my husband, and I too miss having sex. But once I'm in bed, I feel so stressed out that I do not feel the urge to have sex. I just don't know what to do," she explained to the therapist.

Karen was able to work on ways to scale down her responsibilities at work so her life could be less stressful and she could pay more attention to her marriage. There was a good ending to Karen's story, but unfortunately for many couples this often means the end of their relationship.

We all have many responsibilities but we should place them second to the responsibility of maintaining a healthy relationship with the one we love. Think about it this way: If your health depended on maintaining a happy relationship with your love partner, would you make it a priority? Well, in some cases it does. Numerous studies have shown that people who enjoy a healthy love relationship live longer and lead healthier lives. One study shows that an unhappy marriage increases the chances of becoming ill by 35% and can shorten one's life by an average of four years. [74]

3. Have conversations with each other regularly.

Seize every opportunity you get to talk with your mate. This means while eating, while driving, in the supermarket, and other places. This may seem like simple advice, but many people are always otherwise engaged when in the presence of their mates. I am referring to people who sit at the lunch table flipping through a magazine while eating, or to the man who prefers to listen to the radio while driving with his wife. There is plenty of time to do these things when they are alone, so why not take the opportunity to discuss matters of mutual interest when they are together?

At least once a week, make a date to go out for dinner and just talk. What do you talk about? TV talk shows, the weather, the war against terrorism, your boredom at your job, your fantasy about owning your own clothing store, your disappointment with your life, your desire to spend time alone, and whatever else you have on your mind. Bringing your mate up to date with your current thoughts keeps the relationship alive. It also prevents your relationship from falling into a rut by making each other aware of the things that no longer serve the relationship.

I always remember the woman who said to me, "I don't know what happened. Everything was going fine. I mean, we had our differences like everyone else but nothing, so big as to cause him to leave me so suddenly like this." Sometimes it's not the big issues but many small ones that cause the problem. It's the last straw that breaks the camel's back.

Keeping each other current with your thoughts, your dissatisfaction with certain aspects of the relationship, negative thoughts, etc., avoids a build-up of complaints that can overwhelm you both. Remember the purpose of a partnership: One may be good in finding loopholes in financial matters while the other is more sensitive to emotional issues. The partnership runs smoothly when each person brings his/her expertise to the table.

4. Make your partner your most important relationship.

It is extremely important that your relationship with your love partner be the most important of all your relationships. No other relationship should take priority over the one you share with your mate.

"Of course, that goes without saying," you say. Yet I have seen many couples develop other relationships that compete with the relationship between themselves and their mates. Why? Because no matter how special our mates may be, no one person can satisfy your every need for stimulation. Other relationships provide the extra stimulation. A man may find that, no matter how hard she tries, his mate cannot become fascinated by his hobby of collecting model trains, so he maintains a group of friends who share his enthusiasm with his hobby. He may develop close relationships with such friends even when not in the pursuit of his hobby. If your interest or that of your mate shifts away from each other and outside of the relationship, you could be heading for problems.

5. When in difficulty, turn to each other.

Celia found she began frequenting bars and nightclubs with her friends from work. Before they were married, Jim and Celia both enjoyed nightclub hopping; at times, they would stay out until the wee hours of the morning. But Jim lost interest in the nightlife. They went out a few times, but unlike before, it seemed like Jim had to make a special effort to enjoy himself. So when some of the guys and girls from the office suggested they go out for a drink after work, she saw no reason not to go without him.

The trouble came when one of her co-workers began showing interest in Celia and she was enjoying it. Luckily for them, Jim and Celia had a strong relationship. She decided to turn to her husband and explain the whole story. By themselves and with the help of some psychology books, Jim and Celia were able to solve their problem. They were able to understand that the reason Celia was attracted to her co-worker was not because she no longer loved Jim. It was because she had found the missing stimulation she no longer had with her husband. The co-worker was just part of the package. The important lesson to learn from Jim and Celia is to turn to our mates instead of elsewhere whenever we face serious problems in our relationships.

This point should be taken seriously because sometimes we develop close friendships outside of our primary relationships. There is nothing wrong with intimate outside friendships (in many cases, they help us with our primary relationships) but we should not allow these friendships to pull our intimacy away from our primary relationship: You may be familiar with the buddy relationship system women share with their friends. In some cases, they share more intimate information with their buddies than with their husbands. If, for instance, their husbands made a negative comment about their mother, instead of saying, "I don't like it when you speak that way about my mother," they would call their friend to express their dissatisfaction with their husband's actions. If you find that you are more comfortable discussing intimate matters with someone who is not your mate, stop and determine why. It could be a signal of future problems.

The need for social acceptance

Our entire lives are, to a great extent, influenced by the society in which we live. If we were to examine our conscious choice to get married or enter into a long-term relationship, society has an influence on it. We must, however, be aware that left uncontrolled, social pressures can play a major part in the destruction of our marital relationships. For some couples, their life script is already written by their families and societies even before they tie the knot. So although it may seem they are free to choose their lifestyles, they live under unspoken but constant pressure from their families. It would be considered a betrayal, for instance, if the offspring in certain ethnic families decide not to have children.

When Ann Marie, a 28-year-old credit manager for a small company, told her father that, after the wedding, she and her fiancé plan to work part-time and travel around the world for a few years, he suggested that she call off the wedding. He believed they should have children right away.

It is comforting to know that we have the strength and goodwill of our families behind us when we decide to begin a new life with our partners. We know our families would want what is the best for us. And even though we welcome their advice, we (our mates and ourselves) are ultimately responsible for our lives. One of these decisions ought to be our primary relationship takes precedence over everything else.

Building structure

When couples struggle to build a base for their future - the dream house, savings in the bank and planning for children - they sometimes do this at the cost of their marital relationship. They believe it is so important to accomplish these goals that they put their emotional growth, personal development, and desires on hold.

Usually, this happens by mutual consent. So when he says it's more economical to stay at home when she wants to go out for the evening, or when she tells him if she has sex now, she will be too tired to work the night shift at her part-time job, they understand each other. This can result in the loss of passion for the relationship. After a number of years, the couple may become more like business partners than husband and wife.

Some couples survive this period and remain together until they achieve their objectives. But in the majority of cases, they drift apart, sometimes never regaining the closeness they once had.

Somewhere along the way, one or both may feel the pressure and want to slow down. They may realize that they have bitten off more than they can chew, but they feel that it is a sign of weakness to renege on their commitment to each other. Underlying all this is the desire to live up to the expectations of their families and communities. They want to do what is expected of them, so, like soldiers, they proceed to complete their mission.

If such couples had taken time to create intimacy earlier in their relationship, they might have been able to drop their armor and discuss their feelings with each other. They may have realized that sometimes changing your mind is a sign of strength and maturity, and not always a sign of weakness.

During the period of structure-building, one or both parties may find the intimacy they desire elsewhere. Sometimes this leads to sexual gratification outside the relationship, which, at worst, can destroy their efforts to achieve their original objectives.

This situation is not limited to those wanting to build a financial future for themselves and families. Even people who are well established are sometimes driven to further their achievements for various reasons. Sometimes it's nothing more than keeping up with the Joneses.

Chapter Thirteen
Children if and when

It is hardly necessary to discuss the joys and satisfaction derived from creating a new life, then experience the wonder of watching it grow. Who can deny the gratification and hope that the birth of a child brings to a family? But families are wise to avoid being seduced by the idea of having children before they are ready.

A matter of destiny

Most women have been raised with the belief that their life's destiny depends on their ability to create and nurture a family. If a woman is unable to bear children, for medical reasons she believes a part of her femininity is missing. She feels incomplete.

So women often are eager to deliver proof of their ability to reproduce as soon as possible. The longer a woman takes to bear children, the more is her self-esteem threatened. Then there is the question of the proverbial "biological clock."

Like love, parenthood in our society has been over-romanticized, in fact some people believe even more so. Today, many women say they would have a child even if they have to raise the child without a father.

In certain parts of Sweden and Africa, a wife has to bear a

child before her marriage is considered consummated. And even in modern liberated societies, some young couples do not feel married until they have their first child. A woman told me that when two people love each other, the next logical step is to have children. I have known marriage counselors who recommend having a child as part of their treatment to couples in troubled relationships. They convey a misguided assumption that a child would strengthen the bond between them. But the responsibilities that come with creating a new life are so great that families should make a conscious decision to have a child instead of allowing it to happen as a matter of course.

Our ancestral genes give us an instinctive urge to produce offspring. They ensure the survival of the human generation. But as Burnham and Phelan pointed out in their book Mean Genes although these genes served our ancestors well, their importance can be irrelevant in today's society. [75]

For example, our ancestors needed large families to assist them in the occupation of more land. A man's riches were measured by the number of sons he fathered. Sons were more valuable than daughters because they would grow up to be skilled hunters and gatherers. Today, modern inventions and changing social values have eliminated the necessity for large families and we face a problem of world overpopulation. We have seen that in the Republic of China, for example, the law requires that a family has only one child.

So before you convert that extra bedroom into a nursery for your new baby, make sure you have all the facts. Recent studies have shown that many mothers say if they had to do it again, they would not have children. [76] Others say they would have waited a few more years. In almost every case, however, women say that their children have been a source of much joy and happiness in their lives. Even so, some believe their lives could have been much more fulfilling if they had waited or decided not to have children at all.

Also, childless marriages are usually viewed with some degree of suspicion. People tend to think something is physically or psychologically wrong with couples that do not have a child after a reasonable length of time together.

The decision not to have children is a difficult one. To many, the choice not to have children seems unnatural, selfish, self-indulgent, and irresponsible. On the contrary, a decision to wait or not to have children altogether is a responsible and unselfish one, in my opinion, as discussed below.

Do not feel pressured by friends or family members into having children if you decide not to have them. Not having children does not make you less of a person or deficient in any way.

Reasons for not having children

1. You are newly married and need time to develop your relationship.

The intimacy you need to build a sturdy foundation at the beginning of your marital relationship is best achieved in the absence of changes that come with the arrival of a new family member. Couples need time to know and understand each other, so that communication between them (both spoken and unspoken) becomes natural and spontaneous. They may also need a reasonable amount of time alone together so they can fall more deeply in love with each other.

Several studies indicate that the birth of a child puts a tremendous strain on a marriage. Also, friction between couples is likely to increase with the birth of the first child. And relationships tend to get better after the last child leaves home. [77] Most young couples are not fully prepared for the fact that, taking care of children can sap the energy and attention each partner needs to share with each other, especially in the early stages of their relationship.

So even though you both may have agreed to have children, allow time for sexual play and bonding before getting saddled with the psychological responsibility of parenthood. In a survey of 65 divorced fathers, 43 said they did not have enough sex with their partners during their marriage. We must also be aware that men have biological clocks, too. They need to demonstrate their masculinity by fathering an offspring in their image before they get too old. For these reasons, each partner in a relationship must protect the other from falling into the trap of starting a family prematurely, only to have regrets later.

2. You are a career person and raising children would seriously hamper your career.

A woman has the right to exist as a person apart from her role as mother and nurturer of her family. Even though this concept has been accepted in theory, society still expects women to take on traditional roles. For example, in many families, a woman still bears the responsibility of home care even though she works full time outside of the house. They may assist in chores, but both husband and children see home care as woman's work.

Similarly, after a woman reaches maturity, it is expected that her next step is motherhood. Even though they may choose to pursue a career, society and the women themselves believe they have unfinished business with parenthood.

In life, we all have choices, and, yes, women are the only ones in our species who can bear children. But this does not mean that they have to. When I say this, some people ask, "What would happen if everyone was to think that way? There would be no one left in the world?" But this is precisely the point. Everyone does not think this way. To some people, having children may fit in perfectly with their overall life's plan; to others it may not.

Women have made important contributions in the areas of creativity, human, and scientific development. Imagine the losses to society if such women had accepted the concept that their destiny was only to create and nurture a family.

3. Your energies could be better spent pursuing social and charitable activities.

I certainly felt pride and admiration for Heather Mercer and Dayna Curry, two of the eight aid workers who, in 2001 were imprisoned by the Taliban government in Afghanistan before the war started. Imagine the state of mind of these workers being trapped behind enemy lines in such a controversial war - a war in which the enemy proved it would not hesitate to murder thousands of innocent people. It is so easy to lose all hope under such circumstances.

Yet at an interview on CNN after the U.S. Military flew Dayna and her colleagues to safety, she expressed a desire to return to Afghanistan to complete her mission when the war ended. Such dedication to her cause cannot go unnoticed.

Many people have dedicated their lives and resources to assisting others less fortunate than they are. Some of these people are physically and mentally capable of raising a family but they choose not to. Such people should be commended for their unselfish concern for their fellow men.

I once knew a Canadian husband and wife team who spent years in remote areas of Brazil. They were representatives of the Catholic Church and spent their time teaching English and Christianity to local children. Like many others, I presumed they were unable to have children of their own so they sought satisfaction in social work. To my surprise, they explained that even before they were married, they both made a decision not to have children of their own so they could be free to assist needy people in third-world countries. This is yet another example of people who chose an alternative way to serve both God and mankind.

Reasons for having children

Some marriage counselors suggest that couples planning to have a family ought to discuss with each other their individual perceptions of family life. Both partners should share with each other their fantasies of how they picture themselves five to ten years down the road. For example, they need to discuss how many children they plan to have and what style of parenting they intend to use in raising their children. In this manner, some couples may discover that even though they agree in principle on having children, their concepts and expectations of family life vary too much.

If a wide gap exists between your expectations and your partner's, it is best to clarify such matters at an early stage in your relationship. Negotiating differences early can lead to compromises, which may be otherwise difficult to achieve when a problem arises. For example, your style of parenting may be different from that of your partner, but you are able to share opinions where you both may see eye to eye before you are faced with a problem. Sometimes your emotional attachment to the newborn clouds your vision and makes it difficult to see reason when the baby actually arrives.

Here are some answers we received when we asked couples why they plan to have children:

Alice, 36. "I want a family of my own so I won't be alone in the world."

Connie, 28. "I want to have a daughter so we can do things

together, and I can give her all the things I didn't have as a child."

Philip, 37. "I expect my sons will carry on my name and perhaps complete the things I could not finish in my lifetime."

Cheryl, 32. "I have a duty to carry out God's will." "Be fruitful and multiply."

Mary, 26. "I want to have my children quickly so I can quit my job and become a housewife."

Of the 254 couples and individuals interviewed, not one person gave an unselfish reason for having children. Most people focused on the personal benefits they receive from having children. Yet in my opinion, having children can be the most unselfish act a couple could perform.

I believe that every child born is endowed with great potential for making the world a better place for all mankind. We as parents are charged with the responsibility of nurturing and preparing our offspring to take their rightful place in the world. Whitney Houston said it well in her song "The Greatest Love of All"

"I believe that children are our future.
Teach them well and let them lead the way."

If we viewed children in this manner, we would be better able to understand the tremendous responsibility we bear when we choose to create a new life.

I once read about an 18-year-old boy who joined with friends to plan and implement the brutal murder of his father. It reminded me of the Columbine massacre when a group of teenagers systematically planned and carried out an attack with explosives and automatic weapons. They killed several of their fellow students at a Colorado high school in 1999.

Of course, these extreme cases do not occur every day, but

they are the evidence of the fallout from parenting failures.

While I was growing up, I often heard elders in my community say that every child is born with his/her own protection. It took me many years to understand the meaning of this statement.

I now realize that the happiness and contentment that comes with the birth of a child are nature's way of rewarding the parents, thus ensuring the survival of the child. Even in unwanted pregnancies, a mother cannot help but immediately fall in love with her child the moment it is born.

Isn't it remarkable how nature has provided a woman with motherly love? It's the most unselfish form of love that exists, love which is given without the expectation of anything in return. The child is helpless and has nothing to give. Like in animals, Mother Nature has built into females an instinct to unconditionally love and care for their offspring.

Our roles as parents

Mother Nature has done her part. Now it's up to us to complete the job. Let's look at the job description for parenting.

Job description for mothers

- Must be physically and mentally able to provide the love and care necessary for the preservation of life, not only for an infant, but also for a growing child. Will accept a smile or a look of satisfaction on the face of the child as payment for her work.
- Must be able to instill in the child a love for living, not only a wish to remain alive, but also the feeling of goodness to be alive and belief that life is worth living. [78] And since the mother's attitude about life is infectious to the child, a mother must also be a happy person.
- The ideal candidate must do everything in her power to pre-

pare the child to become a completely separate entity, fully adjusted and ready to take his/her place in society. [79] When that time arrives, she must want the child to separate from her - not merely to tolerate the separation, but to want and unselfishly support it.

- Must know she cannot expect anything more for her dedication to her task than the satisfaction of knowing the one she loves will move on and enjoy a happy life.

Job description for fathers

- Must be ready and willing to support the mother in every way, especially during her time of pregnancy and early child rearing.
- Must welcome the task of educating the child in matters that prepare him/her to cope in the real world.
- Must do whatever it takes to provide a favorable environment in which the child learns respect for authority, law and order, and accepted social and economic practices.
- Must also support the separation, when the time comes, trusting he has given the best guidance he could to the child. This should be done with the most unselfish intention only for the benefit of the child.

My doctor once said, "When you and your wife understand the responsibilities you are taking on and still feel that you really, really, really want to have children, go ahead and have them."

Whose needs come first?

Yes, parenting responsibilities should not be taken lightly. However, couples have to take care that the task of raising children does not infringe on their romantic relationship with each other. This is important to mention because, too often, one or both partners become fascinated with the newborn and neglect their relationship with their mates. In some families, the children become more important than the parents themselves. Of course, this is understandable in times of crises (e.g., during illness) when parents rally together and make the child's welfare the number-one family priority.

Many times, however, one or both parents continue to allow the child's needs to take priority over their own or their mate's long after the crisis is over. If the priority given to the child in a time of crisis is never returned to the couple, the relationship becomes emotionally stressful even when both parties agree.

In the initial stages of parenthood, a couple may overlook this stress and console themselves by believing this sacrifice of their happiness is necessary for the benefit of the child. Yet a husband and wife who neglect their own needs in favor of raising their family may find it difficult to regain the intimacy they once shared.

Martha and Jay had their first child when Martha was 37. They both decided to forgo social activities for the first four years unless their child could be included. They made this decision because the child would always cry when left with a babysitter. In a therapy session, Martha said that if she had to do it again, she would have sought another solution because, during those four years, she and her husband drifted apart emotionally. Children are very clever and observant. They may whine, cry, and find other ways to make you feel guilty in order to get their way. If you give into their demands, they will observe that this strategy works and use it frequently until you spoil them.

Judith Siegel Ph.D., in her book *What children learn from their parents' marriage* observes that the relationship between parents is critical to the emotional health and well being of the child. [80] Children learn mostly by example, so the relationship between the parents becomes the blueprint for their intimate relationships. Also, children enjoy a happier childhood when raised in a happy family. So neglecting your relationship with your mate not only robs both you and your mate of your happiness, but also set the wrong example for your children.

Can fathers be caretakers, too?

Studies have shown a high risk of separation and divorce among couples within two years of their baby's birth. [81] Why?

Even though some in our society have accepted the concept of equal rights in a relationship, the mother usually ends up with the responsibility of caring for the child. At first this is okay as most mothers see it as a labor of love. No amount of effort is too much for the newborn. However, when the urgent demands of the newborn and unanticipated problems become overwhelming, she wants her mate to share some of the responsibilities.

This is more accurate for mothers who may have taken leave of absence from their work or given up their career altogether in favor of raising a family. These mothers may even grow to be resentful.

Most fathers usually promise beforehand to assume part of the responsibilities for caring for the child, but get overpowered by the mother who always feels she can do a better job. And since the child is naturally drawn to the mother instead of the father, fathers have to first learn the art of childcare before the mother would leave them alone with the child. [82] The father then falls into the awkward position of thinking he can never get it right, and feels left out of this stage in the baby's life.

His services are not valuable, so he resorts to what he knows best; he channels his efforts in shouldering the responsibility of the increased financial burdens that comes with a new child. He may do this by working harder and longer hours. Of course, many men think earning money to meet the family's needs is more stressful than staying home and taking care of children.

It becomes even harder when a mother has to maintain her job while caring for the children. She may wonder what happened to the equality she and her mate agreed to at the beginning of the relationship. A woman becomes annoyed and frustrated when she cannot count on her mate's assistance in day-to-day caring of the child. Often it is not because he is unwilling to do so, but because she believes he is just not suited for the task.

Such factors can increase the stress level for both partners, and leads to neglecting each other's needs. Each partner becomes resentful and decides to find ways to meet his/her own needs. For example, the mother consoles herself with her new job of being a mother, and the father looks to his work or other ways to make him feel needed.

Parenting as an escape

It is common to hear couples say their marriages were fine until children came along, then they began to fall apart. Some say maybe if they had decided not to have children, they would still be married today.

This is usually not true; children do not break up relationships. But the drastic change that couples experience by this event can strain the couple's emotional resources. In the majority of cases, the break up is caused by problems that may have been subtly ignored in the past. Both partners may have felt something was missing in their lives, and secretly hoped the baby could fill the void.

When a child arrives, some couples seize the opportunity to count on the child as the primary source of joy and personal fulfillment. If you find that you are leaning heavily on your child instead of your mate for emotional support, your relationship could be in trouble. Sometimes one or both parents use their relationship with the child as an escape from marital stress.

It is sometimes easier for a woman to rationalize that the child's needs should take priority over those of her husband by saying, "He can take care of himself but the child can't." The father, on the other hand, feels guilty for acting immature. "Here am I, whining about my needs and trying to take the attention away from a helpless infant." But his emotional needs do not go away. He still needs someone to talk to, someone to share his feelings with, and someone to love him.

He may look for such attention outside the relationship. If he finds satisfaction for his needs elsewhere, he can justify his action by commending his wife for being such a dedicated mother to his child and vows always to support her. If, for example, he finds a woman who gives him the attention he needs, he will tell himself this will only be a temporary solution. His wife will always remain number one and no one can take her place. Of course, we are all familiar with the ending to these stories.

It's your decision

Even though times are changing and couples are considering their personal circumstances when faced with the question of if and when. to have children, a large number of people are still influenced by societies expectations. If a couple were to stop and ask. "Do we really want children?" it would give them a chance to give serious prior consideration to the matter. This in itself can be misleading, however, because it assumes the couple will have all the facts they need to make a sound decision.

The truth is that it is difficult to answer this question accurately because it's hard to predict the consequences of making such a decision beforehand. For example, a couple's situation may change drastically within six years of their relationship. No matter how optimistic or pessimistic your prediction for your future, the reality may prove different. Many women choose to pursue careers instead of having children, for example. After completing their goals, they decided they wanted to have a family although some found it difficult or impractical due to age, medical problems, or other reasons.

When you understand the full implications of creating and caring for a new life, you are likely to be a successful parent. You will understand that children can be a wonderful complement to your happiness, but not the only source. Some parents depend on their children as the source of their life's fulfillment; they live through the children. This puts a tremendous burden on them and can adversely affect their own well-being.

Remember, parents are the foundation on which the family will flourish, so maintaining and strengthening your marital relationship should be number one priority. Parents who enjoy a happy relationship are usually better equipped to turn out well-adjusted children.

Don't allow yourself to be so mesmerized by the patter of your baby's feet that you begin to neglect your relationship with your mate. When you spontaneously follow your natural instincts and dedicate your attention to assisting the helpless ahead of yourself, be careful. It is better to offer assistance from a position of strength rather than weakness. A happy marital relationship provides this strength. Airline companies frequently remind us of this concept. After taking off on a transatlantic flight, the flight attendant reminds you that, in an emergency, you must first secure your own oxygen mask before assisting an accompanying child.

Most people want to maintain satisfying and fulfilling lives. They are prepared to make the sacrifices necessary to achieve their goals. For many, raising a family is one of these goals, and even though it may be one of the most important, we must be careful to maintain a healthy balance with other aspects of our lives.

The sense of security that a child feels in the presence of happy and well-adjusted parents goes a long way in building the child's self-esteem. He/she rationalizes that the parents will always be there for him/her because happy parents are less likely to separate from each other. For people who maintain a balanced life, having a family can be a win win situation. Their lives are fulfilling and their children can grow up to be successful and happy adults. With such knowledge, a couple can relish the thought of having children. They can joyfully look forward to the enjoyment that comes with raising a family.

CHAPTER FOURTEEN
Coping with in-laws

With all the potential challenges new couples face at the beginning of a relationship, it is sad that in-laws can represent an area of negative concern. You might think that people who share a mutual stake in the well being of the person you love are not likely to be a source of problems to your relationship. But many people who have had dealings with their partner's family agree that relationships with in-laws need to be handled delicately.

We've heard it many times: "*When you marry a man/woman, you are also marrying his/her family.*"

What a wonderful feeling to be blessed with the additional strength and support of the family of the one you love. I have never forgotten the warm, comforting feeling I experienced on my wedding night. My mother-in-law looked at me and said, "Welcome, we are now your family." Simple words, but they meant a lot, especially since my own mother had passed away when I was still young. Even until this day, I am still comforted by the feeling of love and support from my in-laws.

In a study of 600 Canadians between the ages of 18 and 60 conducted by Hallmark Canada and *Chatelaine* magazine, 90% said they love their mother-in-law. Nine percent of those surveyed said their relationship with their mother-in-law was closer than their relationship with their own mothers. [83]

However, I have spoken to many people who say their relationship with in-laws has not functioned smoothly. Others report that their in-laws have been a constant source of problems. Judging by the popularity of mother-in-law jokes, we can conclude that problems with in-laws affect more than a handful of marital relationships.

Why is this so? Probably because people instinctively strive to protect their own. Some sisters routinely scrutinize their brothers' girlfriends to see if they meet their standards. And at the first sign of a serious relationship, it is common for the whole family to engage in a microscopic examination of an intended spouse. They value their family member so highly, they want to make sure he/she does not fall into an unhappy relationship.

Although this can apply to all family members, it seems that mothers-in-law feature most prominently in controversies involving in-laws. This should come as no surprise because mothers tend to feel the need to protect their children even in adulthood. Sometimes a mother goes overboard and her good intentions are interpreted as meddling. Couples who understand this can find ways to get along with their mothers-in-law if they wish. In many cases, all it takes is a little understanding and some diplomacy.

A man first leaves his mother and father.
It is only then that he may truly cling to his wife.
—Genesis

This statement from the Bible may be true for parents who have accepted the fact that their children have grown and are now responsible for their own lives. Success in parenting can be measured by the degree of confidence with which the child can separate from the parent. When the child leaves home knowing he/she is ready to take on the world, the parents can pat themselves on the back for a job well done. But not all parents are comfortable with this separation.

Most parents naturally want to maintain a connection with their children, expect them to keep in touch, and to continue to share love and companionship after they leave home. When the child embarks on a new life, however, well-adjusted parents know they have to step back and allow a new life to evolve. Naturally, the parents feel sad when the child does leave the nest, but this doesn't prevent them from giving their support to the new family.

Desperately holding on

Unfortunately, not all parents are willing to let go of their children. Some mistakenly believe their need to maintain control over their children's lives is an expression of their love for the children. Others see the children's departure as a loss of love. They are frightened by the belief that the love they shared with their child will be pulled away and given to the new spouse. This leads parents to come up with creative ways to prevent what they believe to be the loss of love and loyalty, which they feel is rightfully theirs. Such apprehensions manifest themselves in the form of bribery, deception, and downright trickery to the new couple. Some in-laws devote a lifetime to meddling in a couple's lives, and their interference has been known in a worse-case scenario to result in break ups of relationships.

The case of Marjorie is sad but a good example of what can happen when parents go too far in their children's lives.

While studying in medical school, Marjorie, 36, met Francis, also a medical student at the same university. By most standards, Marjorie was considered extremely attractive. It did not take long for the two to realize they liked each other, and they started dating.

Things went well and they made plans to get married after graduation. Francis's parents were financially well off and were of high social standing in their community. They were happy that their son had chosen the field of medicine and already had plans to set up a private clinic for him as soon as he was ready.

Marjorie's parents lived in another city and, though of modest financial means, did not hold a high social position that Francis's parents did. Her father was a professor at a small university and her mother was a high school teacher.

As their graduation date drew closer, Marjorie discovered she was pregnant. Even though he was not ready, Francis proposed to her and they decided to get married. Of course, his parents were not happy with this sudden new development, but gave their blessing anyway. Francis and Marjorie had a happy graduation and were married shortly afterward.

After the wedding, Francis's mother took a keen interest in the new couple's lives, and was personally involved in setting up and furnishing their new home. To Marjorie, this was all new and exciting; being pampered by a loving mother-in-law and a baby on the way made her life very fulfilling. But not long after her son Dennis was born, she began to notice a change in her husband.

Francis began to comment on the way she dressed and carried herself in public. He suggested she needed to improve her public image now that they were both on their way up the social ladder. "It was not the fact that he was trying to change me. What bothered me was the way he did it. I had the feeling that his suggestions were coming directly from his mother. And this was only the beginning. Francis and I began to have regular quarrels and disagreements. We fought about social appearances, family protocol, and child rearing practices. All this time, I knew his mother had been pressuring him to get me to conform to her ideas and social style. This is what infuriated me so much."

Francis's parents were discreet in their relations with Marjorie. They never challenged her directly but tried to get their way through their son. And since the mother exerted tremendous influence on the son, Francis decided it was his responsibility to convince her to be the person his mother wanted her to be. But that did not happen. Instead, Marjorie rebelled and began to have less and less contact with Francis's family to the point that the relationship between her and her mother-in-law became strained. Of course, this produced more tension between her and Francis. During one of their many fights, Marjorie asked Francis why he had changed his views so much about her. How come the way she dressed and carried herself never bothered him before? He said he believed his mother was right and that people should change as their circumstances do. To ease the strain, Marjorie even suggested they move to another city to get away from his parents.

Instead, the situation became worse and Marjorie decided she could not continue to live in such an unhappy marriage. She resolved to work hard and accumulate enough money to separate from Francis. To make things worse, by this time Francis's parents had openly demonstrated that Marjorie would not fit in with their family. This made the relationship with her in-laws almost unbearable.

She never told Francis about her decision to leave him, but secretly made her preparations. Marjorie always knew she could make it on her own. She believed she was a good doctor and that she would not have a problem supporting herself and her child. She also vowed that one day she would gain the respect she deserved from Francis's family.

When Dennis, their son, reached his third birthday, Marjorie announced to Francis that she was leaving him and wanted a divorce as soon as possible. At first, Francis protested but when he realized Marjorie had already made her decision, he agreed to start divorce proceedings.

Marjorie and Dennis said goodbye but maintained contact with Francis until the divorce papers were finalized. They then disappeared and neither Francis nor his family knew anything about the whereabouts of Marjorie and her son.

It may be reasonable to suggest the true reason for this breakup was rooted not in the actions of the in-laws, but in the fact that Francis did not stand up to them. Yes, Marjorie might have been disappointed when Francis took sides with his mother because this was a side of her husband she had not seen before. Even so, these problems could have been worked out under different circumstances. But the powerful influences from her mother-in-law exerted on her son weighed heavily against the couple's chances of their relationship surviving.

When parents' influences prevail

Even though adult children may know their relationship can pay a high price for parents' intervention, sometimes the rewards are too enticing to ignore. Everyone likes an easy life so it becomes difficult to say no when your father or father-in-law offers to groom you for vice president of his lucrative company. This is even more true if we believe we could not achieve such heights in a similar company on our own.

We may even work three times as hard as anyone else to justify our position. But we may always feel it would have been better if we had achieved the position on our own merit. We may also feel a sense of obligation to our parents, which can impair our dealings with them. For example, we may feel guilty if, for instance, we want to make our own vacation plans instead of accepting our parents' invitation to spend it with them.

Some parents use the fact that their child is involved in the family business to exert control over the relationship. Some parents do not hesitate to let their daughter-in-law know she is enjoying all the comforts of life because of them. Imagine the kind of stress this can cause between couples.

Hooked on love

It's common to hear of instances when children who were raised without love grew up to be unhappy adults. It may surprise you, however, to learn that many children who were raised by loving parents also become adults with unfulfilling lives. Some parents love their children too much. They shelter them from all harm; they seek to shield them from suffering or inconvenience; they declare their children's happiness is of the greatest importance to them.

As adults, we may begin to rationalize that our parents' motivations for giving us too much were actually to satisfy their own needs. Looking back at our past, we can begin to see how much of our lives were spent trying to make our parents happy. We did so in an effort to return the love that was so freely given to us. We may not have fully understood the impact of our parents' actions while growing up, but it became evident when we decided to live separate lives from them.

It can become difficult to kick the habit of dependency on our parents. When we need financial assistance, fight with our partners, and need a shoulder to cry on, or when we need business advice or a job referral, where do we turn? Of course, we may have to endure their criticisms and listen to their lectures, but in the end, they will do whatever they can, to avoid letting us down.

According to some behavioral scientists, we pay a hefty price for such love. [84] In therapy sessions, people confess they are tormented by feelings of inadequacy. They know they should be able to stand on their own without their parents' help, but no matter how much they try, they end up at their parents' doorsteps. They become hooked on the goodies even though they pay a high price. And like the credit card trap, it is easy to ignore this at the time they receive the goods, but deep inside they know that "when you dance to the music, you have to pay to the piper."

Marjorie's story continued

Marjorie lived alone with her son and went on to do her post-graduate studies. Her determination to prove to her former husband and in-laws that she was capable of reaching whatever heights she wanted drove her to strive for higher achievements. Instead of just practicing medicine, she discovered she enjoyed the field of medical research. She did well and was responsible for the publication of a paper on her research subjects.

Francis had also excelled in his field and was the head of his own clinic, which specialized in gynecology. He had married a woman who was unable to have children for medical reasons. The marriage lasted three years and Francis was now single again. One of the main reasons cited for the divorce from his second wife was constant interference from Francis's family.

This was about eight years later. Dennis was now 11, but Francis hadn't seen him since he was three. People close to his mother were fascinated with Dennis' striking resemblance to his father.

Marjorie was one of the attendees at a medical convention held in a big city. Francis also attended without knowing Marjorie would be there. Even during the first leg of the convention, they were not aware of each other's presence because the meeting room was large and it was a full house.

When they broke for lunch, though, Francis spotted Marjorie. You can imagine the surprise on both their faces when they greeted each other. But Francis was in for a bigger surprise.

The two had been talking for less than two minutes when Francis's eyes shifted to a little boy walking in their direction. His countenance changed immediately, his mouth opened, but he was speechless. Marjorie turned to see Dennis approaching her. Francis did not move. There was instant recognition. Francis was shocked by his son's resemblance to him. He could not hold back the tears that came to his eyes. Dennis had accompanied his mother to the big city and had waited in the hotel's lobby to have lunch with her. It was a happy day for all of them.

Five months after that eventful meeting I spoke to Marjorie who told me she was in constant communication with Francis. He had taken a special interest in Dennis' life; they did many things together. I wanted to know if they had plans to get back together. She said, "I have since had a few relationships with other men, but I never found the kind of connection I shared with Francis. I realize how much I loved him. Even so, I could not return with him despite his many proposals for us to reunite. I believe what we had together was destroyed by his parents."

It's up to you

It would be nice if all stories of marriage break ups could have happy endings, but reality tells a different story. It is true that parents love their children and want the best for them. But sometimes their lack of knowledge and over enthusiasm produce harmful results. Perhaps, if parents were to know beforehand the pain and suffering that can result from their interference, they might act with more moderation in their behavior toward their sons-in-law and daughters-in-law.

Since there are no such guarantees though, couples must take steps on their own to:

- Avoid from the beginning potential problems with in-laws.
- Deal with problems as soon as they arise.

Understand their expectations

Sometimes it is difficult to know how problematic your relationship with in-laws can be until you become part of the family, and then it's too late.

When you marry her son, a mother may accept you as one of her daughters or even the daughter she never had. This could be comforting, even flattering. But watch out. She may have unrealistic expectations of you. It is easy to see why you would go out of your way to be accepted by your new family. But you have to set your own limits. This is more evident if, for example, you marry into a family in which the culture or religion may be different than your own. You may politely go along with their traditional practices without knowing how much would be expected of you. You may later become resentful as more and more demands are made. It is better to understand what is expected of you before you agree to go along with any new practices.

Here are a few signs to watch out for:

1. Your mother-in-law is overly aggressive in including you in her plans. "I've already spoken to my dressmaker; whenever you are able we can stop over and take your measurements for a new dress for the upcoming party."

Evasive strategy: As courteously as you can, let your mother-in-law know that you like to select your dressmaker personally. "How kind of you, Shirley. I appreciate your interest but I already have one of my own."

2. Your father tries to get you to influence your husband to name your first son after him. Your response: "How sweet of you, Dad, but Jack and I had a name picked out over a year in advance."

3. Your father constantly makes offers to loan money to your husband, most times with strings attached. "You can get a good deal on a house here in New Jersey. I know a few builders who owe me favors. If money is a problem, don't worry. We can work things out"

Your reply: "It's very kind of you to offer, Dad, but Jenny and I have a standing agreement not to buy a house until we are more financially comfortable. In any case, we plan to stay in Michigan for a while."

4. You notice your mate has difficulty saying no to his/her parents. This could be a sign that he/she may have left home physically but not psychologically. Parents may continue to exert great influence. It may be wise to point out you would prefer a life separate from his/her family. Let him/her know emphatically and as early as possible in the relationship that you will not tolerate his/her family's intrusion on your affairs. Do so before your mate develops a pattern of leaning on his/her family for support. Sometimes this problem could have deeper psychological roots. If you believe this to be the case, you will be well advised to seek professional assistance alone or together.

Your reply: Honey, you know how demanding your parents can be, but now that we have separate lives from them, we have to give priority to our affairs. Let them know you are always willing to help, but now you also have other responsibilities.

5. Your husband spends too much time at his parent's house and

tries to get you to do the same. Your mother-in law always has some special dish that he likes. "I'm making his favorite lasagna today, if you don't have time to eat it here, you can stop by and take it home with you."

Your reply: Mom, you know we both love your lasagna, but we already had lunch and made dinner plans. If we take it home, it will only become leftovers.

This is a common occurrence in families who have maintained close ties with each other. At a luncheon after a two-day work seminar, my colleague Gino ate very little. When I asked him if he was on a diet, he said, "No my mother is expecting me for lunch." I then said, "I guess your mother's cooking is the best in the world." He replied, "That's exactly what I keep saying to my wife."

Leaving home is not always easy

Some people believe that, after the ceremony, newlyweds can kiss their parents goodbye and go on to form their own family unit. This does not happen automatically or instantaneously. Remember, the ties with parents existed from the day you were born and won't disappear easily. Also, true bonding with a new spouse is not achieved overnight. You may have accepted your mate as "the one," but you will need time to be absolutely sure you have made the right choice. During this period of uncertainty, you naturally look to your parents for security. Your parents would do whatever it takes to make you happy, but you do not yet feel this way about your mate.

The important thing to remember here is that you, not your parents or your mate, are responsible for your happiness. A good way to achieve independence from parents is to join forces with each other. Your mate needs to know your motives are sincere. For example, your partners must not believe you are jealous or simply don't like his/her parents. Say, for example, "I understand that, like me, you have a close relationship with your parents. But the time has come for us to form our own family unit." It is better for your mate, to be the spokesperson when dealing with his/her own parents in this matter. But knowing that you together are a team backed by loyalty and support, your mate can confidently communicate with his/her parents. Here's what he/she might say:

1. "I have decided it would be better for my relationship if my wife and I keep our lives separate from yours."

2. "This does not mean that we intend to completely sever ties with you. We shall maintain close contact and will always be there for you whenever necessary."

3. "I have chosen (your wife's name) as my lifelong partner and she is completely with me all the way. She also loves and respects you both, and as the saying goes, 'You are not loosing a son, but gaining a daughter.'"

Protecting your relationship

Sometimes the problems with in-laws have deep roots and you may not be able to side-step certain issues, no matter how hard you try. Before you know, you can be immersed in ding-dung battles, screaming matches, and the sense of helplessness in your relationship. For some couples, this becomes a way of life and may eventually be the cause for the break up of their relationship.

Use strategy to counter attacks from in-laws

Your mother-in-law perceives you as the enemy without getting to know you. It is common for your mother-in-law to see you as her competitor for her son's love and attention. She may then take steps to let you know who the most important person in his life is, who is the boss (the mother of course). For example, she calls your house often and asks to speak directly with her son. Or in your presence she speaks to her son as if you were not there.

Some wives in this position react by complaining to their husbands or threaten to insult their mothers-in-law. In some cases, the husband is slow if not reluctant to confront his mother, having been brought up to believe that such actions would be a sign of disrespect. The wife is then left with a feeling of helplessness and may begin to take her frustrations out on her husband.

Tania, 39, a housewife, talks about her battles to gain respect from her mother-in-law. "Imagine asking me to step aside so she can use my photographer to take pictures of her family at my wedding ceremony. After the wedding and it became clear to me that my husband would not stand up to his mother, I decided to take matters into my own hands. Without my husband's knowledge, I called her up and invited her to have lunch at a restaurant. After eating, I came directly to the point. I asked her why she treats me like a non-person. We talked for two hours. We talked about her, about her son and about me, and even though she was not specific, I had the feeling she had had some misconceived ideas about me. I say this because from that day onward, our relationship changed for the better. Even my husband could not understand what had brought about the change. Now I get along well with my mother-in-law and have fewer fights with my husband."

A little communication can go a long way. Perhaps your mother-in-law has a genuine problem with you because of something you said or did. If this is so, it is better to find out early. It might be a simple misunderstanding, something you may be able to nip in the bud.

When your partner is not supportive

Perhaps the greatest downside in the in-laws problem is the bitterness it causes between husband and wife. People who may have otherwise gotten along well find themselves close to the start of World War III when in-laws enter the picture. But more often than not, the lack of support from your partner is much more painful than any attack from your in-laws.

Said Kim, "I know Neville trusts my judgment usually, but it drives me crazy that he doesn't believe me whenever I tell him what his mother does to me when he is not around." Kim, a part-time secretary, went to see a therapist when she had nowhere else to turn. Her mother-in-law pretended to be nice to her when her husband was present. The moment the husband's back was turned, the mother would criticize and insult her. It's as if she had a Jekyll and Hyde personality. Her husband thought she hated his mother, and even suggested Kim might be mentally disturbed. Fortunately, her therapist believed her story, and suggested she use a tape-recorder to capture her mother-in-law's voice on tape. Her husband was stunned as he listened to the recording of his mother's voice.

Some sons grew up believing that their mothers would always want the best for them. As a result, they find it hard to believe their mothers would do anything to harm the one they love. They rationalize, "There has to be some misunderstanding somewhere."

Knowing how her son may react, a mother may choose not to discuss with him what she perceives as her daughter-in-law's faults. She may reason that his vision is impaired by love and cannot be trusted. But mother knows best, and it's her responsibility to protect her son. So she seizes every opportunity she gets, like pulling the daughter-in-law into the kitchen for some girl talk. She says, "Do you think this is the way to keep a kitchen? My son is not accustomed to untidiness; you'd better get your act together."

It hurts even more if you are finally able to provide proof of his mother's attacks on you and he does nothing about it. You may even think he is beginning to question your competence. For example, it could be devastating if you disagree with him and he floors you with a statement like, "Maybe mother was right."

If this describes you, whatever you do, do not lose your self-esteem. Remain confident that you are not the guilty party. It is easy to doubt yourself when your partner in whom you placed your trust takes sides against you, even his own mother's side. When the situation gets to this stage, the solution lies with you and your partner. You cannot depend on your mother-in-law to change her attitude toward you. In fact, it can develop into a, "who's wrong and who's right" tug-of-war with you in the middle. I know of a case in which a woman who was being abused by her husband got no sympathy from her in-laws because they said she was the one who provoked it.

Get your partner to listen

Keep in mind that even if your partner feels his/her parent's behavior toward you is out of line, he/she may not welcome your attacks. No matter how badly they might have behaved, most people will not tolerate an attack on their parents, even from a spouse. You have to proceed carefully.

The first thing to do is get your partner's attention. This sometimes proves difficult and more so if your mate has already begun to take sides with his/her parents while questioning your competence as a partner. You, more than anyone else, would know how to get your partner's attention, so choose your words carefully. Comments like, "When are you going to act like a man and stand up to your parents?" or "If you don't smarten up, I am leaving," should not leave your mouth, even though you may have them in mind. Ultimatums and abusive statements only add fire to fury.

Be specific. As you begin to speak, you may find your partner has that "no not again" look on his/her face and is ready to dismiss you. For example, instead of saying, "Your mother is too nosey and I can't stand her," you can say, "Your mother insists on knowing how much money I spend on the things I buy for our house." Instead of saying, "Your father is a total idiot and does not know how to treat people," you may say. "Your father offends me when he makes abusive statements to me in public."

You must let your partner know exactly how your in-laws' actions affect you and that you need his/her assistance in finding a solution to the problem. As a team, you stand a better chance of changing the situation than as separate individuals.

When you have done your best

If you were to marry into a family of happy, well-adjusted people who live satisfying and fulfilling lives, you probably won't have in-law problems. Also, if your partner decides to stand up to his/her parents, letting them know you come first, you can handle even the worst in-laws.

But in most cases, the reality is different. Sometimes, even before formalizing a relationship with our partners, we can sense we are about to enter into a battle zone with in-laws. Even so, we may ignore remarks like, "I don't see why my son has to rush into this marriage now." "I always pictured my daughter being married to a doctor, but I guess things don't always work out the way you want them to." Or "How are you going to take care of your family if you plan to keep your job?"

Such remarks may be just passing comments, but could also be a signal of future trouble. You may ignore them because you believe that-

- Once you are married and your in-laws get to know you better, things will be all right.

- You are marrying your partner, not your in-laws, you can't be bothered what they think of you.
- You can play along with them, making them believe you are the person they want you to be just to keep the peace.

Try to learn as much as you can about your partner before falling in love with. But sometimes you can never be prepared for your partner's reaction when he/she relates to his/her parents. Veronica, 32, a lab technician married Mike, 38, who ran his own construction company. "I was shocked to see how sheepish Mike, behaves when dealing with his parents. He just can't say no to them. We had to postpone our plans several times because Mike's parents needed something or other. Remember, this is a guy who runs his company like a boot camp and won't tolerate excuses from anyone. You can imagine my surprise when I first learned how much control his parents had over him."

Relationships between most people and their parents are complex. So is the relationship between two spouses. Put them all together and you have an even more complex situation. Psychologists say that parents' refusal to let go of their children could be an indication of their belief that the child has not yet reached the stage of maturity necessary to make his/her own judgment. [85] They say, "My child is not yet capable of making an intelligent selection. It is therefore my duty to continue to guide him/her."

Also, your siblings may base their rationale on the following: "We are the most important ones in your life. Now that you have selected someone else to replace us, it is our responsibility to make sure you have chosen the right person."

When you come right down to it, a lot of the conflict involving in-laws relate to jealousy. Your siblings may see your relationship as a loss of first rights to your love and attention, now that you have someone close to you. But most in-laws are well intentioned. And even though some of their actions do not reflect this, you as a daughter or son in-law, must keep this in mind when dealing with them. Remember, they cannot be that bad if they were able to produce and raise a child able enough to meet the standards you set.

How great it would be if you could convince your in-laws that their son or daughter has made the right selection in a life partner; and that your presence improves their offspring's life. But sometimes, your in-laws' attitude does not improve. If you are satisfied that you did the best you could, that is enough. No matter how skillful you might be, you may not be able to get through to them. Some people are simply impossible to reach. Therefore your most important goal is to protect what is most sacred to you, your relationship with the one with whom you have chosen to spend your life.

Chapter Fifteen
Epilogue

Preoccupation with money

One of the major causes of unhappiness in people's lives is money. "Money can't buy happiness." "Money can't buy love." "Money is not everything." Everyday, people are in a mad scramble to earn more money. Yes, we need to earn money to provide for our survival, but for most people, the more they have, the more they need. Many people across North America spend at least 40 hours a week at jobs they say they don't particularly enjoy. Yet, many say they would work more hours if the opportunity to earn more presents itself.

People get caught up in the eternal struggle for money because they believe money will bring them happiness. Unfortunately, for many people, it's only after they acquire money that they realize they still feel unhappy. Some people never succeed in reaching their financial goals, so they continue to live unhappy lives blaming their unhappiness on lack of money. Someone once said if you were to take all the money in the world and divide it equally among all the people both rich and poor, within a few years the money will end up in the hands of the same people who have it now. If this were true, it would support my belief that many people need to have money to appreciate that money does not necessarily make people happy!

A final observation

While traveling on the streets of San Juan Puerto Rico several years ago, I saw a sign written in bold letters on the wall of a building. It was written in Spanish and the translation read something like this: "Life is what you are doing now while you're waiting for what you really want."

I began to imagine the thoughts of the writer who thought it necessary to share his/her wisdom with others. But even before then, I realized that most people I met lived their lives dreaming of a better tomorrow. As average Americans go about their daily struggles, dreams of winning the lottery, buying that dream house, or going on luxurious vacations are often on their minds.

There is nothing wrong with dreaming of the future; in fact, it provides a great incentive for people to better themselves. The trouble is that we have become experts at planning for the future, but find it difficult to enjoy what we have today.

Why does it take a close encounter with death or the diagnosis of some terminal illness for us to stop and take a look at our lives? Why do we have to wait until we come to the end of the road to look back and appreciate all the good things life has given us? Wouldn't it be better to really enjoy these things while they are happening? Why can't we enjoy the moment?

About 25 years ago, I was sitting with friends in a fine restaurant. As we savored the fine cuisine, one friend said, "I want us to realize how special this moment is for all of us. Many years from now, we will look back and recall what a good time we had tonight. I say, let's voice our appreciation now so we can enjoy the true value of this moment." I saw the value in his comments then, and through the years I have known many people who have made ambitious plans for the future. Many of them succeeded in achieving their goals but some confessed that things happened so fast, they couldn't fully enjoy their moments of success.

Here's how it goes. First you say, "All I need to do is to graduate from college, find a decent job, then I'll be happy." So you finish school, find your job, but realize you would be happier if you become the manager of your department. So you struggle do achieve the position of manager. Now you say, "It's great being manager. All I need to put the icing on the cake is to buy that new Mercedes Benz." Then the house, the property by the lake, and so on. During this time, you do not place much value on your achievements so far because you see them as a stage you need to go through to achieve what you really want. But when you have accomplished most of the things you wanted, you still do not feel fulfilled. Then you wonder where the time went. More frightening than that, you may have lost your incentive to be happy.

Don't let this happen to you. Prepare for the future but live for the moment. As the saying goes, "Live every day as if it's your last because one day it will be."

The End

Notes

Introduction

[1] Centers for Disease control and Prevention, The report *First Marriage Dissolution, Divorce, and Remarriage*, report issued (November, 2001).

[2] U.S. Census Bureau, *Marital Status and Living Arrangements,* (March, 1996), P20-496.

[3] Noel Hornor, *Living Together: What Aren't They Telling You?* United Church of God, an International Association (2002), http://www.ucg.org/articles/gn41/living.html

[4] Helen Fisher Ph.D., *Brains Do It: Lust, Attraction and Attachment*, published in Cerebrum, a Dana Forum on Brain Science (Volume 2, Number 1, Winter 2000).

Prologue

[5] Statistical Abstract of the United States: 1998, Page 111, Table 156; Statistical Abstract of the United States: 1972, Page 63, Table 86; and National Vital Statistics Reports, August 19, 1998.

[6] David Popenoe, Ph.D., and Barbara Dafoe Whitehead, Ph.D., *The State of Our Union: The Social Health of Marriage in America* (June, 2000).

[7] See survey Questions. Appendix.

[8] See survey Questions. Appendix.

[9] Sharon Lerner, *Good and Bad Marriage, Boon and Bane to Health*. (NYT) 22, 2002, Tuesday. Late Edition - Final, Section F, Page 5, Column 2.

Chapter One

[10] Nathaniel Branden, *The Psychology of Romantic Love,* Bantam Books; ISBN: 0553275550; Reissue edition (May 1, 1985) Page 119.

[11] Rich Rahn, *Beliefs Are Not Facts*, This article was excerpted with permission from his book, *Evolve Yourself*, published by Duh! Books, Bloomfield Hills, MI http://www.innerself.com/Creating_Realities/beliefs.htm

Chapter Two

[12] Anthony Robins, *Unlimited Power,* published by Simon and Schuster New York. Page 184.

Chapter Three

[13] Gary Clark, *Your Bride is in the Mail*, http://www.planet-love.com/gclark/order.php

[14] Gary Clark, *Your Bride is in the Mail*, http://www.planet-love.com/gclark/order.php

[15] 1. Robert J. Scholes, PhD., with the assistance of Anchalee Phataralaoha, *The mail-order Bride industry and its impact on U.S. Immigration*, MA. 2. Glodava, Mila, and Richard Onizuka, *Mail-Order Brides*: *Women for Sale*, Alaken, Inc. (Fort Collins – Colorado, 1994).

[16] Glodava, Mila, and Richard Onizuka, *Mail-Order Brides: Women for Sale*, Alaken, Inc. (Fort Collins – Colorado, 1994).

Chapter Six

[17] Lee A. Lillard and Linda J. Waite, *The work is documented in Til Death Do Us Part: Marital Disruption and Mortality*, RP-487,1996 (reprinted from *American Journal of Sociology*, Vol. 100, No. 5, March 1995, pp. 1131-1156).

[18] Howard Markman, Ph.D., professor of psychology and director of the Center for Marital and Family Studies at the University of Denver, says, "*Money is the number one thing that couples fight about in America.*" Also, Markman, Stanley, Fiske, and Mellan , issue of Money Magazine from the cover feature story, *Is Money Ruining Your Marriage?* (March, 1999).

[19] 1. Jennifer Wolcott, *Finding the path to a lasting relationship*, Staff writer of The Christian Science Monitor 2. Dr. Neil Clark, *Partners for Life*, (Warren Nov, 2001). 3. Nathaniel Branden, *The Psychology of Romantic Love*, Bantam Books; ISBN: 0553275550; Reissue edition (May 1, 1985), Page 117.

[20] Nathaniel Branden, *The Psychology of Romantic Love*, Bantam Books; ISBN: 0553275550; Reissue edition (May 1, 1985) Page 117.

[21] Helen Fisher Ph.D., "*Most people who get divorced remarry 75% of women and 80% of men remarry. Half of these remarry within three years of divorcing.*" (1994).

[22] Nathaniel Branden, *The Psychology of Romantic Love*, Bantam Books; ISBN: 0553275550; Reissue edition (May 1, 1985) Page 101.

[23] Branden, Page 112.

[24] Branden. Page 112

[25] Journal of Sex Research, Vol.38, No.2, I*nvoluntary Celibacy: A Life Course Analysis,* and *Surfing for Sex: Studying Involuntary Celibacy Using the Internet* appeared in Sexuality *and Culture,* Vol.5, No.3, (University of Georgia, Summer 2001).

[26] Patrick Zukeran, *Principles for Dating*, a research associate, and a national and international speaker for Probe Ministries. (1900 Firman Drive,Suite 100 Richardson, TX 75081) Tel. (972) 480- 0240 Fax (972) 644 – 9664 info@probe.org

Chapter Seven

[27] Donatella Marazziti, *Falling madly in love may really make you mentally ill*, the research found emotional and biological similarities between people in love and those suffering from a psychiatric disorder, says a report in New Scientist magazine (University of Pisa, 1990).

[28] Helen E. Fisher, Ph.D. *Brains Do It: Lust, Attraction and Attachment*, this article published in Cerebrum, a Dana Forum on Brain Science (Volume 2, Number 1, Winter 2000).

[29] D. Marazziti, DH Akiskal, A. Rossi, and GB Cassano. *Alteration of the platelet serotonin transporter in romantic love*, (Published in Psychological Medicine, 1999), Vol. 29: pp.741-745.

[30] Andrea N. Jones, *Marriage, Monica, Mores, Motherhood, Myth And Mystery* , Pacific News Service, (660 Market Street, Room 210, San Francisco, CA 94104, 12-03-99), tel: (415) 438-4755. Jinn Magazine:<http://www.pacificnews.org/jinn

[31] CNN Evening News and World Report, (Nov 22 2001).

[32] Halle Berry and Russell, Crowe were the top winners at the 8th annual Screen Actors Guild Awards Sunday night in Los Angeles, Speech: Halle Berry's speech. 74th Annual Academy Awards, http://www.oscar.com/oscarnight/winners/winner_actress.html

[33] Norton, Arthur J., and Louisa F. Miller, *Marriage, Divorce and Remarriage in the 1990's,* U.S. Department of Commerce, Economics and Statistics Administration, Bureau of the Census, Current Population Reports, Special Studies #P23-180.

[34] See survey Questions. Appendix.

[35] John Gray.Ph.D., *Mars and Venus Starting Over*, a Practical Guide for Finding Love Again After a Painful Breakup, Divorce, or the Loss of a Loved One, Mars Productions Inc. New York.

Chapter Eight

[36] "Ira Reiss Premarital Sexual Standards in America, New York:"

[37] Permissiveness with affection, Reiss 1960.

[38] *Enter Promiscuity, Exit Fidelity Why Do Men Cheat On Their Wives?* Are Hard Days Killing Our Nights Softly? 2001 NriGate.com.

[39] Hall and Zhao, *Cohabitation and Divorce in Canada*, Journal of Marriage and the Family (May 1995), 421-427.

[40] DeMaris and MacDonald, *Premarital Cohabitation and Marital Instability: A Test of the unconventionality Hypothesis*, Journal of Marriage and the Family, (May 1993) 399-407.

Chapter Nine

[41] Terry Burnham and Jay Phelan, Mean Genes, Perseus Publishing, (Cambridge, Massachusetts, August 2000), Page 177.

[42] Jennifer Roback Morse, *Love and Economics*, Published by the Hoover Institute by the board of Trustees of the Leland Stanford Junior University. (copyright 2001) Adapted from the new book, *Love and Economics: Why the Laissez-Faire Family Doesn't Work*, published by Spence Publishing Company, Dallas, Texas (www.spencepublishing.com). Available from the Hoover Press.

Chapter Ten

[43] Jacqueline Olds and Richard Schwartz, *Marriage in Motion,* Publisher: Perseus Book Group, ISBN: 0738208302; (August 23, 2002) Introduction, Page XVIII.

[44] Nathaniel Branden, *The Psychology of Romantic Love*, Bantam Books; ISBN: 0553275550; Reissue edition (May 1, 1985) Page 150.

[45] John Gray, Ph.D., *What Your Mother Couldn't Tell You & Your Father Didn't Know,* J.G Productions Inc. (1994), "Why Men stop focusing on Relationships." Page 295.

[46] Kostiuk, P.F. and Follman, D.A.1989. Learning curves, personal characteristics and job performance. Journal of Labor Economics (D.A.1989), 7:129-146.

[47] John Gray, Ph.D., *What Your Mother Couldn't Tell You & Your Father Didn't Know*, J.G Productions Inc. (1994) "When Women are Providers" Page 321.

[48] John Gray, Ph.D., "Nurturing the Female Side." Page 102

[49] John Gray, Ph.D., "Nurturing the Female Side." Page 102

[50] Masters & Johnson, *Sex and Human Loving* (1998).

[51] Greg King, Senior Relationships Counsellor/ Domestic Violence Prevention Worker, Relationships.Australia, Brisbane, Queensland. *User Friendly Journeys to Self Mastery: Working with the Emotionally Impoverished Male.* Section: "Linking at the "outer" to reclaim the inner." This report can be located at. www.law.gov.au/aghome/commaff/lafs/frsp/mensforum/people/26.htm

[52] Francesca Cancian, *Love in America,* (Cambridge, England: Cambridge University Press, 1987), page 82.

[53] William Masters & Virginia Johnson, and Robert Kolodny, *Human Sexuality*, second edition, (Boston: Little, Brown, 1985), page 247.

[54] CNN News and World Report, (Jan. 10. 2000).

Chapter Eleven

[55] Helen E. Fisher, Ph.D., *Brains Do It: Lust, Attraction and Attachment*, this article published in Cerebrum, a Dana Forum on Brain Science (Volume 2, Number 1, Winter 2000).

[56] Jonathan Kramer, Ph.D., and Diane Dunaway, *Why Men Don't Get Enough Sex & Women don't Get Enough Love,* Pocket Books. New York. "Good Girls, Bad Girls" Page 61.

[57] Rebecca Kodat, *How do fish breathe under water?* Copyright 2001 by PageWise, Inc. http://papa.essortment.com/howdofishbrea_rlyl.htm

[58] Riane Eisler, *The Chalice and the Blade* (New York: Harper & Row, 1987).

[59] J. G. D. Clark, *Mesolithic period or Middle Stone Age, period in human development between the end of the Paleolithic period and the beginning of the Neolithic period.* (1953, repr. 1970).

[60] Irene Elia, *The Female Animal* (New York, Henry Holt, 1988), page 255.

[61] Irene Elia, *The Female Animal* (New York, Henry Holt, 1988), page 255.

[62] Helen Fisher, *The Sex Contract: The Evolution of Human Behavior*, (New York: Quill, 1983), page 223.

[63] Helen Fisher, *The Sex Contract: The Evolution of Human Behavior,* (New York: Quill, 1983).

[64] *The art of loving* Erich Fromm. Harper Collins. Pub. Inc. Page 49.

[65] Edward O Wilson, *On Human Nature,* (New York: Bantam Book, 1979), page 89.

[66] Nathaniel Branden, *The Psychology of Romantic Love,* Bantam Books; page 145.

[67] *Midlife Sexuality with age. Getting better with age,* Source: Oasis Mayo clinic In an article Web site http://lifx.com/midlife_sexualtiy_and_women.htm.

Chapter Twelve

[68] 1.Nathaniel Branden, *The Psychology of Romantic Love,* Page 133. 2.Study by Dagmar Pescitelli, analysis of Carl Roger's theory (1996), www.wynja.com/personality/rogersff.html

[69] Constance McKenzie, M.Ed., M.A., NCC, MAC, CBCC, CBAT, Specializing in depression, *Anger: What is it? And Why,* Copyright © 1994-2002 by Pioneer Development Resources, Inc.

[70] Hankins & Hankins 1998; Ellis, 1992.

[71] Mark Gorkin, *The four faces of anger,* Pioneer Development Resources, Inc. LICSW 2, 2002.

[72] Dr. Davis, professor of educational psychology at the University of Wisconsin-Madison, *Article #34 from R&D Innovator Volume 2, Number 4,* (April 1993).

[73] Jacqueline Olds and Richard Schwartz, *Marriage in Motion,* Publisher: Perseus Book Group; ISBN: 0738208302; (August 23, 2002) Introduction, Page XV.

[74] Canadian Government's Health Canada. The Canadian Health Network. *Our Relationships influence our Physical health,* Article prepared by the British Colombia Council for Families (October 2002).

Chapter Thirteen

[75] Terry Burnham and Jay Phelan, *Mean Genes,* Perseus Publishing, (Cambridge, Massachusetts, August 2000), This is the subject of the book.

[76] 1. Terri Casey, *Pride and Joy: The Lives and Passions of Women Without Children*, Published by Beyond Words, (1998), ISBN: 1-885223-82-X 2. Anne Petrie, *Gone to an Aunt's: Remembering Canada's Homes for Unwed Mothers,* Published by McClelland and Stewart, (1998), ISBN: 0-7710-6971-5.

[77] Ohio State University. Press Article # FLM-FS-7-98, *Parenting: A Circle of Life.*

[78] Erich Fromm, *The art of loving*, Harper Collins. Pub. Inc. Page 46.

[79] Erich Fromm, *The art of loving*, Harper Collins. Pub. Inc. Page 48.

[80] Judith A. Feeney, Lydia Hohaus, Patricia Noller and Richard P. Alexander, *Becoming Parents,* (Published by Cambridge University Press, copyright the authors, 2001), pp. 12-18.

[81] Annette Erlangsen and Gunnar Andersson, *The Impact of Children on Divorce risk in first and later marriages,* MPIDR Working Paper WP 2001 – 033 page 3, results.October 2001. Max-Planck Institute of Demographics Research. www.demogr.mpg.de

[82] Rose Allen, *Gender Differences in Parenting*, the University of Minnesota Extension Service. Regents of the University of Minnesota.

Chapter Fourteen

[83] Chatelaine Magazine, Article Archives (1999).

[84] Laurie Ashner and Mitch Meyerson, *When Parents Love too Much*, William Morrow and Company. Inc. New York. "The Silver Platter" pages 27-35.

[85] Chana Heller, MSW, *Letting Go: Notes From a Mother,* as a teenage daughter leaves home, one mother panics, takes stock

and lets go. Is the mother of five children, ages 11-20. She works for Aish HaTorah Los Angeles as the Director of Womens Outreach and has taught Jewish Parenting Workshops for 8 years. She is married to Rabbi Dov Heller, also of Aish HaTorah LA.

Appendix

Survey Questions

The survey consisted of 254 questionnaires filled out by men and women randomly selected across various U.S. States and Canadian cities. Personal interviews were conducted with 80 respondents. The ages of people surveyed ranged from 25 – 40 years. We asked general questions about marriage and relationships, and the people we personally interview were given a chance to verbally elaborate on their answers. It was most important to get personal reactions from respondents.

Sample questions:

1. What is the most important ingredient for a successful relationship?

2. Are you presently happy in your relationship?

3. Would you choose the same partner if you had to do it again?

4. What was the most important quality that made you choose your present mate?

5. Would you ever marry again?

6. Do you think your partner changed after you got married?

7. Are you disappointed with the way your marriage turned out?

8. If you had to do it again, what are the two most important things you would do before you get married?

9. What "qualities" do you consider important in a mate?
    - Physical Attraction
    - Sexuality
    - Money
    - Intelligence
    - Sense of Humor
    - Self-confidence
    - Career Success
    - Other
10. Would you marry a woman you meet in a bar?
11. Who should pay for a date, the man or the woman?
12. How do you feel about a wife who works outside the home?
13. Do you think providing for a family is a man's responsibility?
14. Do you think housework is a woman's responsibility?
15. Do you plan to have children? If so, how many?
16. Would you marry a man or woman who already has children?
17. Do you regret having children?
18. What were your reasons for having children?
    - The normal thing to do
    - Family pressures
    - Biological clock
    - My partner wanted children
    - Love Children

19. Do you think men and women know what they want?

20. Do you feel casual sex is okay?

21. Would you marry a woman who had sex with you on the first date?

22. How often do you have sex with your partner?

23. Do you believe people should hold off on marriage until they find their soul mate?

24. Do you believe you could love someone at first sight?

25. Do you believe you could find true love the second time around?

About the Author

A college graduate in journalism, Peter Hector majored in Creative Advertising and launched a career in market research. For Love is No Guarantee, he headed a team of research assistants who conducted interviews in several U.S. and Canadian cities.

An entrepreneur and avid traveler, Peter has visited 44 countries. He has provided personal coaching to individuals on marriage and other issues since 1998. He himself has been happily married for 10 years and lives with his wife Diomira in Toronto, Canada.